THE
AGE OF
INFLUENCE

THE
AGE OF
INFLUENCE

THE POWER OF **INFLUENCERS** TO ELEVATE YOUR BRAND

NEAL SCHAFFER

HarperCollins
Leadership

An Imprint of HarperCollins

Published by HarperCollins Leadership,
an imprint of HarperCollins Focus LLC.

Book design by Aubrey Khan, Neuwirth & Associates

ISBN 978-1-4002-1637-6 (eBook)
ISBN 978-1-4002-1636-9 (TP)

Library of Congress Control Number: 2019948542

Printed in the United States of America
20 21 22 23 LSC 10 9 8 7 6 5 4 3 2 1

CONTENTS

ACKNOWLEDGMENTS

Every book that I write is special, and *The Age of Influence* is no different. With previous books, I approached the topic by trying to avoid being influenced by others and their thoughts. With this book, I accepted the fact that influencer marketing and the concept of influence has been around for a long time, so I wanted to take advantage of that fact and truly stand on the shoulders of giants and use others' industry experiences to uncover new insight. For that reason, this book is also my longest undertaking, spanning more than two years from concept to publication. I simply couldn't have completed the task without all of the support and inspiration from so many around me.

My first thanks must go to my wife and children, who always supported me when I had to meet critical deadlines or interrupt family time in order to create more content. Our mutual family love is the foundation of what I do and why I do it. I also have my parents to thank, as well as all of my brothers and sisters-in-law, who have always supported me in various ways over the years.

I must also thank and state that this book simply would not have been written without the incredible support I received from Lee Constantine at Publishizer.

I also want to thank everyone at HarperCollins, who put their trust and confidence in me to write this book, as well as their extended editorial staff. I also want to thank my own staff, who helped me in various ways to develop the content in this book.

A special thanks to all of the institutions of higher learning that have recruited me to help in the education of executives in all things digital business, most notably Rutgers Business School, Irish Management Institute, and the University of Jyväskylä.

There are numerous mentors in the social media and marketing industry who have also inspired me in many ways, directly and indirectly, and have contributed to my understanding of marketing, to which I hope this book contributes, in a similar way. There are too many to list, but I did want to mention a few who have inspired me. Seth Godin for sharing so much knowledge that is truly evergreen and as relevant today as when he wrote it. Michael Stelzner for his and Social Media Examiner's support of me as a speaker at their Social Media Marketing World conferences. Fellow Rutgers Business School instructor Mark Schaefer, whom I first shared this book idea with many moons ago and who encouraged me to write it. Jay Baer for being an incredibly inspiring and awesome individual. Brian Solis for continual inspiration on helping me answer the question, "What's next?" Mari Smith for selflessly and graciously sharing her knowledge with the world. Joe Pulizzi for being the Godfather of content marketing and educating so many through his content. Ann Handley for encouraging me to write and inspiring my goofiness at the events where I am lucky to see her. Dan Gingiss for enlightening me on customer experience marketing, even if he is a Cubs fan (GO DODGERS!). Gary Vaynerchuk for his chutzpah and telling it how it is, literally inspiring a whole generation of entrepreneurs like me. Mr. Likeable Dave Kerpen for his inspiration and friendship. Michael Brito for all things social business and especially employee advocacy (not to mention his similar passion for my Lakers). Chris Brogan for being one of the most intelligent and down-to-earth authors you'll ever meet. Lee Odden for all that he and his company have done in the influencer marketing space. Jenn Herman for inspiration on everything Instagram since the social network launched.

Finally, there is another list of people whom I need to acknowledge because they actually invested in the creation of this book through my pre-order campaign on Publishizer and remained supportive and patient while they awaited the publication of this book. These individuals and organizations invested in me long before a publisher was found, and I can't thank them enough. There are many of them, and since everyone's investment, no matter how small, is a precious one, the only fair way to thank them is to list them all here in alphabetical order: Pasi Aaltola and everyone at the University of Jyväskylä, John Althoff, Maraya Altuwaijri for your incredible support over the years online and offline, Andrea Armstrong, Steve Arnold, Bill Ashton for helping me in my travels, Julien B., Fabiana Baumann, Stefan Beckert, Leonardo Bellini, Natalie Benamou, Yuri Bilyarov, Sherry Bonelli, Robert Burns for your continued friendship over the years, Jeffrey Buskey, Sinead Carroll, Jessica Casamento, Annie Chang for all of your support and engagement over the years, even though we have yet to meet IRL, Bonnie Chomica, Emma Cox, Stephen Curtis, Bonnie David for all of your engagement and support, Karen DeSantis, Victoria Desemone for your inspiration and being a friend, Kathy Doering, Liz Dorland, Steve Eisenberg for all of your engagement and support, Darrell Ellens, Kari Embree for your support ever since the Maximize Your Social days, Mike

Falconer, Salvatore Fallica, Gwendolyn GaBree, Julie Gallaher, Robert Geller for all of your collaboration and contributions over the years, Sean Ghazanfari for your friendship and support, David Goldsmith, Richard Haagensen, Ryon Harms for inspiring me inside and outside of social media, Rune Haugsoen, Simon Hewat, Lynn Hoban, Lori Holly, Brian Honigman for your professional inspiration and support, Toni Hopponen and Flockler, Jeffrey Howell, Mana Ionescu, Natalie Jacks, Cheryl Johnson, Martin Jones for your incredible support and friendship, Erika Kessler, Marcus Kirsch for your fellow author support, Dino Kuckovic and everyone at Falcon.io in Copenhagen and throughout the world for supporting me, Pramod Kunju, Werner Kunz for your support and inspiring the education of professionals in digital marketing, Serge Labelle for your friendship and similar love for Japan, Rene Lisi, Robyn Maka, Aine Mc Manamon, Mary Beth McCabe, Suzie McCarthy for supporting me over the years, Doug Morneau, Niklas Myhr for your support and continuous educating of professionals on digital marketing here in Orange County as well as in Sweden, Norman Naylor for your incredible friendship throughout the years, Jonathan Nunez, Nicolette Orlemans for your continued support, Kuenyoung Park, Lory Passov, Jennifer Radke, Tatiana Richards for your support since I began networking locally, Jon Rivers, Maria Rodriguez and everyone at Open Influence for their incredible support, Greg Russak, Jo Saunders for your support from Down Under, Karin Sebelin for putting your trust in and supporting me, Liron Segev, Juhli Selby for your continued friendship, Semi Semi-Dikoko, Ravneet Singh, Joe Sinkwitz and Intellifluence, Yao Sun, John Sustersic, Valentina Tanzillo, Michael Taubleb for supporting my speaking business, Susan Thompson, Mark Tietbohl, Mike Turner, Maurits van Sambeek, Robert Varipapa, Guy Vincent for launching Publishizer, Vala Vincent, and

ACKNOWLEDGMENTS • xi

Byron White for supporting me as a speaker at the Content Marketing Conference.

It truly takes a village to write a book, and my work is only as good as the love, friendship, support, and inspiration I received from all of the people above and so many others that I simply don't have enough space to thank. For everyone else, thank you from the bottom of my heart.

Neal Schaffer

INTRODUCTION

Several months ago, when I was in the market for a new phone, I went to my local T-Mobile store in Southern California. While going through the upgrade process with the salesperson, the inevitable question came up: What do you do for a living? That's not always a quick question to answer. My work as a marketing educator and consultant means I have many roles, including as a public speaker, an author, or even working as an influencer. What makes this question more difficult is the general misconceptions that surround influencer marketing.

It was surprisingly easy to answer the question this time. In the modern-day gig economy, people often have multiple jobs. It turned out the salesperson was a local-level influencer himself who worked with nearby businesses to demonstrate the most effective ways for them to engage with influencers at events for business benefits.

In many ways, this interaction highlights why I've written this book.

Social media marketing has been around for over a decade. With few exceptions, brands are still challenged by it. Business profiles on social media have been around since the days of MySpace, but companies still tend to advertise to their consumers over social media instead of engaging them.[1] Many company Twitter accounts still tweet in ad-speak. The same mistakes are still being made by companies that don't understand the fundamental nature of social media. Despite all the marketing conferences and how-to blog posts that marketers read, the content they produce still pales when compared to influencers. The constantly changing landscape of social media means that despite all the money poured into platforms for advertising, campaigns are finding increasingly less traction in organic ways.

For many people, Instagram models and YouTube gamers are some of the most visible influencers today, but to assume all of influencer advertising runs through them is to lose sight of the ball at the start of the game.

Being an influencer is not about merely taking selfies, putting them online, and then getting paid thousands of dollars from brands to mention them. Influencer marketing is not about paying someone else to take selfies and put them online. It is about engagement and communication. It is about building relationships. In many ways, I don't consider the leading names often associated with influencer marketing as influencers anymore: They have priced themselves out of the equation, shown that their endorsement is money-driven, and have, in effect, become a new form of media.

The term "influencer marketing" is poorly understood. This development of big-name influencers becoming their own media doesn't particularly clear the waters. Considering only these top-rung social media users as influencers is a fundamental misunderstanding of what influencer marketing entails.

Humans are social creatures. We learn from each other. Individually, we learn from our greater society. How we communicate is always changing. We have communicated and influenced each other in decision making since the beginning of civilization. Early cave paintings of indigenous peoples around the globe have been found to be maps and recommendations on where to hunt certain animals, information to be passed down to others.[2] In many ways, the printing press kickstarted society as we know it today. It fundamentally changed communication, allowed for mass publication, and ushered in the Industrial Revolution and the development of cities and plenty more societal phenomena. In recent decades, the ways we communicate have changed with incredible speed through mass communication, the telephone, and the internet. Social media has changed this again. Failing to adapt to new communication methods will leave your message unheard.

In recent years, many books, podcasts, blog posts, and TED talks have discussed the best ways to build your social media presence or to develop influence on a personal scale. Many blueprints for developing your personal brand have been published. *The Age of Influence* does not do that. While part of this book discusses how to grow more influential on social networks, my focus here is on engaging the voices of influencers, "leveraging the other" as I call it, to spread your message. It's investing what power you have to move outside and incite word-of-mouth marketing so that "other" voices will talk about your business. It is not about merely building brand but giving you the tools to engage influential voices for a variety of business objectives. It is about returning to the original premise of engaging in social media: inciting word-of-mouth conversations about your brand.

Social media represents the convergence of information and communication. More people are both communicating through and consuming information on social media. Communication has been democratized. Everybody has reach on their chosen social network. Everybody has a platform to connect with those who share similar interests. Businesses are realizing the value in leveraging other social media users such as employees, brand advocates, or influencers to help spread their message.

Just as my phone salesperson built his following and a platform where he is influential, coaching local small businesses on engaging with influencers, nobody's online profile is necessarily as they seem. To customers, he is a phone salesperson. To his employer, he is an employee. To his followers, he is a trusted voice to be listened to. The online persona of everyone around you cannot be judged from a single glance. While some translate well from the physical world to Twitter or Instagram, others do not. A leading CEO who might command a room of thousands at a conference might not have a voice online. However, his or her employee could have a following of millions. To paraphrase George Orwell's *Animal Farm*: All social media voices are equal, but some are more equal than others. Engaging with those whose voices are being heard is essential to spreading your message online, rising above the digital noise and creating meaningful relationships. Even though social networks rise and fall, this principle remains. *The Age of Influence* covers this principle of learning how to engage and build actual relationships online.

In my travels around the globe for conferences and clients, I have found that influencer marketing is more prominent in Southeast Asia and China than anywhere else in the world. The rise in consumption of media over the now easily accessible smartphone that traditional media did not keep pace with in those regions parallels the unprecedented growth of smartphones leaping over fixed-wire technology much more quickly and broadly there than in Western societies. The accompanying democratization of media influence there has been filled through bloggers, YouTubers, and Instagrammers, in addition to the influencers who have built communities across native Chinese social networks such as WeChat and Weibo.

Businesses in that part of the world really understand how much power these influencers hold. Revenues generated from influencers in China are thirty times greater than that in Europe.[3] Half of the top ten fashion brands on the leading Chinese online shopping site Taobao were launched by influencers.[4] A brand I met in Singapore—a large conglomerate that manages many consumer-facing brands—was launching a new beauty brand. As they put it: If we want to get the word out about our new brand, how else would we do this but with influencers? Relying on traditional advertising and forms of brands for a legacy brand is one thing, but when launching a startup, sidestepping those gatekeepers and connecting directly with your consumers has a much stronger benefit.

Many businesses started out with word-of-mouth marketing without really knowing it. Happy and successful customers told their friends, who told their friends, and so on. When communicating on social media, the way to incite word-of-mouth marketing is not from the declining reach of your organic posts or your advertisements. It's about leveraging people.

Think about it: What if you shifted your investment of time and money from paid ads and paid social to joining the conversation with customers who have some influence on social media? What if you invest your organic social budget in relationships with people? This returns to the connection between customer success marketing and social customer service. People rule social media and always will.

I am reminded of a study published some time ago in the *Harvard Business Review* that highlighted the myths about what brands think customers want. As you continue reading, you will see how influencer marketing is a natural solution for these ideas proven false through the data in the study.[5]

1. **Most consumers *don't necessarily* want to have a relationship with a brand.** Social media is the domain ruled by people, and its users are increasingly creating deeper relationships with influencers, not brands.
2. **Shared values, *not interactions*, build relationships.** Brands garnering more engagement in social media doesn't necessarily mean they are building relationships with people. Influencers are building relationships by being authentic and attracting others who share their values and perspectives.

The interaction with my phone salesperson highlights that businesses still don't understand how to interact with influencer marketing. It's entirely possible that his company is unaware of the influence he yields. As an employee, and a direct customer-facing employee, his affinity for the brand and knowledge about the product is a resource that is being drastically underutilized. This type of personal and knowledgeable voice in marketing content is powerful. When done right, harnessing employees' ideas for content creation and encouraging them to be more active on social media as part of an employee advocacy program can be powerful. This is a point that many brands and businesses have not yet grasped.

Elements of influencer marketing have been around for decades in many ways. Celebrity endorsement is one of the earliest ways of leveraging voices to spread your brand's message. Affiliate marketing and advocacy marketing have been part of many brands' strategies for years. Translating these to the digital age can be tricky. Who do you target? How do you approach them? How do you guarantee returns on time and monetary investments? Digital platforms are new playing fields.

Social media will always be in flux. This is the inherent obstacle. The rules frequently change. New platforms rise. The newsfeed algorithms get revised again. Social networks come and go. It's impossible, and ill-advised, to stretch yourself across all of them. The sudden growth of visual social networks like Instagram launched a new generation of influencers who are distinct from their blogger, YouTuber, or even Twitter predecessors. Influencers can cover the increasingly difficult visual ground for you much better than you can yourself, while sidestepping the problems of mastering new and rising platforms, or worrying about a platform's longevity.

Harnessing true people power—and that is what the voices of influencers are—requires a different approach to how you've traditionally spread your brand's message. Influencer marketing is a shift in communicating and interacting with your customers and audience. It's also able to deliver results far, far beyond those traditional returns. It's about user-generated content. It's about community. It's about relationships. It's about engagement. It is more than just spreading a message. This is the next generation of social media marketing.

PART ONE

WHY INFLUENCER MARKETING?

Before we plunge into advice on how to leverage influencer marketing, we need to fully understand the paradigm shift occurring in mass communications that is enhancing the value of word-of-mouth marketing through influencers. Establishing this baseline understanding will help bring you up-to-speed as to how I see the potential that influencer marketing has for every business.

This all begins by understanding the digital climate of today.

The very essence of how messages are spread has shifted. Engaging with the masses has changed. Brands are already leveraging influencers to achieve marketing objectives. Influencer marketing is one of the fastest-growing methods of spreading a message about a brand—and for good reason.

The ROI from influencer marketing is clear. In one survey, nearly 90 percent of all marketers found ROI from influencer marketing comparable to or better than other marketing channels (see Figure 1.1).[1] Another case study showed ROI on influencer marketing to

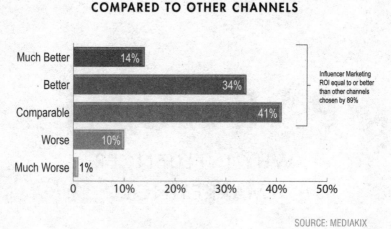

**INFLUENCER MARKETING ROI
COMPARED TO OTHER CHANNELS**

SOURCE: MEDIAKIX

Figure I.1

be as high as eleven times the return on traditional digital marketing options such as banner ads.[2]

With strong social media platforms globally and ubiquitous smartphones that can easily access them, everyone could be a publisher if they wanted. Everyone could have a platform, an audience, or community—including businesses. At the same time, while consumers now steer away from traditional advertising messaging, with 74 percent of consumers using one or more strategies to avoid advertising all together, they are influenced by the online media they see from people they follow and trust.[3] This trust is tied to the emergence of online influencers, which has led to rapid growth in influencer marketing (see Figure I.2). The older methods of engaging with celebrities don't translate well to the new personality of influencers.

As the world catches on to the significant returns from influencer marketing, spending on influencers increases. The market for influencer marketing on Instagram alone is estimated to grow from less

INFLUENCER MARKETING ROI 11x OF DISPLAY AD

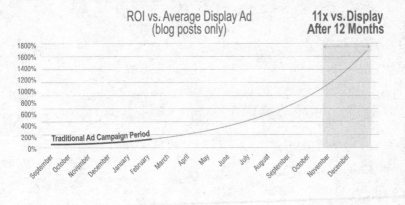

SOURCE: IZEA / TAPINFLUENCE

Figure I.2

than $1 billion in 2015 to as high as $16 billion in 2020 (see Figure I.3).[4]

As a percentage of global advertising spending, $16 billion is still a small amount—but it may prove to be only the tip of the iceberg in terms of spending on influencer marketing.

INSTAGRAM INFLUENCER MARKETING GLOBAL SPEND

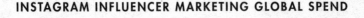
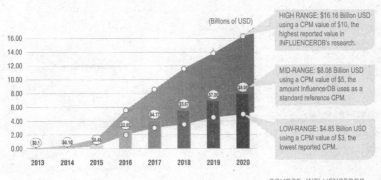

SOURCE: INFLUENCERDB

Figure I.3

THE ORIGINS OF INFLUENCE
IN THE MODERN WORLD

While *influencer marketing* has become a popular buzz-word in today's marketing circles, the fundamental concept has been prevalent in marketing throughout history. Tapping into the power of someone with authority, an audience, and followers to spread one's message is the foundation of marketing. The ways people consume their messaging and the ways those who hold influence communicate have changed over time. The present state of digital media has transformed the ways people communicate and the ways your message can be heard. Influencer marketing encompasses strategies to engage people with your message in a more trusted manner with a longer term perspective.

• • •

THE HISTORY OF INFLUENCER MARKETING

The concept of leveraging celebrities or those with influence to endorse or promote a product has been fundamental for centuries. In the 1760s, Josiah Wedgwood impressed the Queen of Great Britain, Charlotte of Mecklenburg-Strelitz, enough with his new form of earthenware that she gave him permission to call it Queenware, making it the first documented endorsement.[1] The approval of the royal family certainly helped Wedgwood establish itself as a brand of choice.

When John Jaques and Nathaniel Cook designed a new set of chess pieces in 1849, they approached the English chess master Howard Staunton to write about the set in his newspaper column.[2] Having a current chess master endorse the chessmen in his column would be a coup in spreading the news about their new design. It went even better than planned: Staunton was so impressed with the pieces he not only covered and endorsed them but derided other designs. Eventually this early celebrity endorsement broadened, to the point where Staunton signed the sets as they were sold and received a royalty from each sale. The pieces are still the standard used in competition chess today.

In the late 1800s, companies began to print trade cards to include with their products. For instance, famous actors such as James Lewis and Mrs. G. W. Gilbert were shown in one of their best-known stage roles—but holding a bottle of Ayer's Sarsaparilla.[3]

British-American actress Lillie Langtry was linked to multiple brands including Pears Soap.[4] Mark Twain lent his name to cigars and other tobacco goods.[5]

THE RISE OF MASS MEDIA
AND INFLUENCER MARKETING

The twentieth century rise of mass media including radio and television allowed for all marketing, including celebrity endorsements, to become much more widespread. Tobacco companies were early adopters of the format with James Stewart and Ronald Reagan endorsing brands like Chesterfields.[6] Athletes like Babe Ruth also endorsed tobacco products.[7] Alfred Hitchcock endorsed Western Union telegrams for swift communication from on-set.[8]

One of the most visible product endorsements, and one that undoubtedly changed the approach to sports endorsements, was the partnership between Nike and Michael Jordan. Nike had a stronghold on the track and field shoe market but were strangers to the basketball market when they signed Michael Jordan in 1984. The visibility of Jordan and his on-court accomplishments helped Nike grow to the brand we know today. Jordan's position and devotion to his role as the face of Nike reached something of a watershed moment during the 1992 Olympics. The Team USA uniforms were sponsored by Reebok. Jordan felt that he shouldn't stand on the dais to receive the gold medal while wearing a competitor's logo. Instead, he went into the crowd before the medal ceremony and asked fans for flags from the USA to drape over his shoulder, obscuring the Reebok logo.[9]

The Jordan signature shoe changed the playing field for sports brands in the early 1980s. Before then, most NBA players wore the same Chuck Taylor All-Star shoe no matter how big of a player they were, from Bill Russell to Wilt Chamberlain, Magic Johnson to Julius Erving. Now close to twenty active NBA players have signature shoe lines. Even non-athletes have signature shoes, such as Kanye West designing sneakers with both Nike and Adidas.[10]

PEOPLE TRUST PEOPLE

People trust people—that's the principle at work here. Humans are social beings. We communicate with people, even when it's online and digital. We trust people over messages from companies, corporations, or brands. Nielsen finds the most powerful and relied-on source of trust comes from people, with 92 percent of people likely to trust a recommendation from a friend.[11] The next most-trusted source (70 percent) is consumer reviews online, another form of listening to a trusted person. Editorials by editors, authors, or journalists were the third most trusted source.

For brands, garnering trust means winning business.

The Edelman Trust Barometer clearly spells out the importance of trust and its impact on our purchasing decisions as consumers.[12] When consumers were asked about their deciding factor for doing business with a brand, trusting the brands was the fifth popular response after key product attributes such as quality, convenience, value, and ingredients.

How does a brand best gain the trust of consumers in a digital-first world? Celebrity endorsements were the traditional choice because they make it easier to align your brand with elements of the celebrity's image and their popularity. The glamor and power of the celebrity's identity and brand transfers to the product. It's success and class by association. It's easy to trust a current chess master on the best kinds of chessmen. It's why Nike had a $1.6 million increase in the golf market because of its ties to Tiger Woods, despite a scandal that caused other sponsors to drop him.[13] Jordan's continuing celebrity and brand as an all-time basketball great means Nike continues to release Jordan shoes and sell astronomical numbers despite the fact Jordan hasn't played an NBA game since 2003.

Celebrity power lasts because it's based on people with authority. This is where influencer marketing enters the picture and is beginning to compete with celebrity endorsements for marketing budgets. Edelman Trust Barometer looked at the 18–to–34 predominately millennial demographic and found that not only was relatability to a given influencer twice as important to their popularity or celebrity status, but also a whopping 63 percent trusted what influencers said about products more than what brands say about themselves.

It should then come as no surprise that in a more recent study, 82 percent of consumers said they were very likely to follow the recommendation of an influencer they follow, which shows that trust translates digitally.[14] Twitter has even reported that users trust influencers nearly as much as their own friends.[15]

Clearly the ancient concept of trust combined with advances in digital technology has brought upon an incredible transformation of how we decide who to do business with and who influences us in our purchasing decisions.

HOW THE INTERNET CHANGED INFLUENCE

We've seen the internet change how people communicate and get information. Specific knowledge is now gained with great speed, and communication happens at an unprecedented rate. Over the last decade, social media has fundamentally changed how people communicate, streamlining social interaction while lowering barriers between everyday people. Smartphones mean online access from anywhere at any time of the day, not just at home or in the office. The ease of content creation, publication, and distribution has democratized fame modeling, and hundreds of thousands of influencers have emerged. Celebrity status isn't required. A person can claim status as an Instagram celebrity simply because they have thousands of followers.

At the same time, studies show certain groups of consumers trust celebrity endorsements less than before.[16] Celebrity endorsements won't go away or fade completely—they've been a tentpole of influencer marketing for over a century. Some of the skepticism comes from celebrities not aligning with their own identity and the engagement clearly being an ad. Celebrity influencers have received backlash, also, for when the endorsement comes across as not natural. In the case of the Fyre Festival, the influencers were paid for their promotion of the festival without disclosing that their posts were ads.[17] The spectacular failure of the event reflected back on the influencers whose credibility then took a hit. The skepticism came from the impersonal, transactional nature of the engagement.

Minority groups in particular are becoming wary of traditional celebrity endorsement. Brad Pitt may be a film star, but his endorsement can be pointless if your brand aims for a smaller demographic that doesn't connect with, or trust, a Hollywood actor. As a result, more people are turning to alternative sources for information they trust. Some of these are bloggers and "everyday experts"—people the consumer identifies with on a personal, friendly basis, someone "more like me." The rise of the "mommy blogger" phenomenon is an example of this. For a brand wanting to connect with new mothers, engaging with an "everyday influencer" in a niche market like mommy bloggers might bring far more benefits than an association with a Hollywood star. Google itself has already stated that, for millennials who spend a lot of time watching online videos, YouTube stars are already more influential than traditional celebrities.[18]

All of this is driving influencer marketing in a new direction. More than two-thirds of millennial consumers value peer endorsement over those from celebrities.[19] As influencer marketing begins to mature and see the value that non-celebrity "peer" influencers bring, it is no surprise that 94 percent of marketers now think that transparency and authenticity are key to influencer marketing success.[20]

An agency manager handling the #IGNITEYourCity influencer marketing campaign for the running shoe company Puma said it best: "We felt that actually getting those real life runners in our target markets speaking for Puma would be a more authentic way to deliver our message than simply putting out promotional material."[21]

New companies have emerged to help marketers discover, engage, and measure activities associated with influencers in this new landscape. The sheer number of potential influencers forces us to scale beyond human capabilities to better understand many social media users' influence over a wide range of communities discussing almost anything imaginable. These same tools help you target the demographics important to you. Engaging a celebrity endorsement from Brad Pitt would be a game-changer for most companies, but it wouldn't suit every brand or product from a target audience, cultural alignment, or budget perspective. Tapping into these smaller markets is more powerful for niche brands. You can reach further through harnessing the influence of everyday experts with powerful influence over unique communities.

Influencer marketing can engage both celebrities and noncelebrities. The concepts in this book are applicable to anyone with a platform and an audience. Social media has democratized both media authority and its influence. The influencer is seen as more trustworthy because of their authenticity, or their "everyday person" type of testimonial. The rise of networks like Pinterest and Instagram that cater to more specific demographics, along with the prevalence of YouTubers and bloggers with opinions suited to smaller and more precise audiences, has shifted marketer and consumer attention to micro-influencers.

It's no longer vital to aim for the largest demographic. Targeting specific audiences open to your message can be more efficient.

THE ADDITIONAL BENEFITS OF INFLUENCER MARKETING IN THE AGE OF SOCIAL MEDIA

Would encouraging people to talk to their friends about your product or brand organically over coffee each day add to your marketing campaign? If they talked to their friends in social media about your product, the viral power of that communication would only work to your benefit.

Engaging with an audience through influencer marketing strategies has the same effect. While leveraging influencers for traditional time-limited marketing campaigns is still widespread, there is greater value in establishing relationships with influencers to build a larger social media community. People share your message on social media to a whole field of people they influence whenever they interact with your brand on a regular basis. Over time, organic engagement with your product increases, and you will successfully leverage other people including consumers, employees, advocates, and friends into helping spread your message through the channels that most people spend most of their online time in.

Influencer marketing is the extension of a tried and tested form of marketing that works. The popularity of social media and resulting democratization of influence has transformed the way companies need to adapt in order to continue to reap its benefits.

Nordstrom shows us what the future might look like for those that adapt. One study showed that four out of every five of mobile web visits and nearly 40 percent of desktop visits to retailer Nordstrom.com's site that were referred from another site were driven by an influencer.[22] But are they just visiting or are influencers actually influencing purchasing decisions?

The results of a recent survey by global e-commerce company Rakuten paint a clear picture of how the resulting digital democratization of influence has influenced purchasing.[23] Of the 3,600 shoppers surveyed in the United States, Europe, and Australia, 61 percent interacted with an influencer daily and 35 percent multiple times a day. Nearly 90 percent of surveyed consumers said they were inspired to make a purchase based on what they saw from an influencer, and 80 percent actually made a purchase recommended by an influencer by clicking on the link or image. When probed further for details, 74 percent of consumers surveyed spent up to $629 on a single purchase that was inspired by an influencer they follow.

All of this data indicates that these trends provide unparalleled opportunities for marketers who can tap into the growing commercial influence of this new generation of digital influencers. If nearly three-quarters of luxury goods purchases, whether they take place in physical stores or online, are influenced by what consumers do online, you can begin to gauge the enormous potential influencer engagement has for your brand.[24] That influence will only grow as McKinsey has estimated that in the long-term, what consumers do online will influence 99 percent of online *and offline* purchasing decisions.

THE EMERGENCE OF DIGITAL AND SOCIAL—AND THE IMPORTANCE OF CONTENT

What we refer to as influencer marketing is not a new idea. What's different now is the landscape, the medium, and the method. The rise of social media and the content-centric nature of the media we use to communicate have shifted the ways in which we receive information. It's changed who and how we trust.

Technology has always changed how people interact and communicate with each other. This extends to communicating brand messages. Companies used to hire the traveling salesman to take a brand's message door-to-door to connect more directly with customers than the mass communication of newspapers, radio, and television could. The shift to telemarketing and cold-call marketing couldn't have happened without the phone being adopted in households. Digital marketing through emails and search engine optimization (SEO) began to take hold in the late 1990s when the internet became adopted in households. The rise of social media marketing is the latest manifestation.

CELEBRITIES AND MORE

In recent years, Instagram has shown the largest growth in user adoption, perhaps because of the refreshing way users can easily interact with visual content. Humans are visual animals. It should be no surprise, then, that in the current climate, Instagram is leading the field. The investment into Instagram advertising is already in the billions of dollars, with a significant percentage of this undoubtedly going to influencer marketing.

What's interesting here is that the money is not all going to celebrity endorsements. Non-celebrity influencers have developed followings of well over a million users in a way that makes them valuable voices. The top five non-celebrity earners in a recent report were Elenora Pons, Huda Kattan, Cameron Dallas, Sommer Ray, and Zach King.[1] Most of these names mean nothing to the general population. For their followers, for the communities that they've built and the areas of interest in which they engage, these people are huge. The top five each have over 20 million followers and can demand up to $144,000 per Instagram posting.

Seeing these names and figures leaves many people asking: Just how did this happen? How are everyday people making tens of thousands of dollars for simply publishing one photograph?

Marketing has always been about getting your message in front of your target audience. It's always been about knowing where your audience is, what they're looking for, and where they're looking for it. The most apparent example of this was the innovation of the billboard: Brands knew exactly where their audience would physically be and put the message in front of them. It took some research and insight into finding where the message would be most effective—household cleaning items were most effective on neighborhood billboards, while office typewriters were better on metropolitan trains—but the message was put in front of the right demographic. As the audience shifted to digital platforms, advertising migrated, too.

In December 2017, for the first time digital ad spend surpassed television ad spending globally (see Figure 2.1).[2] In 2019, it is predicted that digital advertising in the United States will finally surpass that of all traditional advertising (television, radio, print) combined, less than thirty years after the launch of the first web browser.[3] Just like a majority of consumers, a majority of marketers are now beginning to think digital first.

Digital spending has not plateaued, either. It will continue to grow while TV ad spend stagnates (see Figure 2.2). Consumers and audiences now have a different relationship with television viewing. Network television is no longer the only way people watch television shows. Many streaming services have removed or limited ads, meaning advertising has had to find

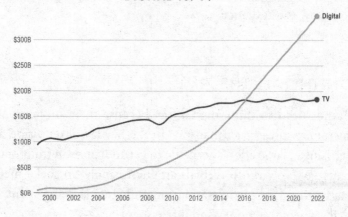

**GLOBAL AD SPEND:
DIGITAL vs. TV**

DATA FOR 2017 AND BEYOND ARE FORECASTS   SOURCE: MAGNA / VOX

Figure 2.1

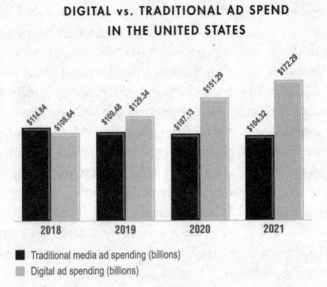

DIGITAL vs. TRADITIONAL AD SPEND IN THE UNITED STATES

- ■ Traditional media ad spending (billions)
- ▨ Digital ad spending (billions)

SOURCE: EMARKETER

Figure 2.2

other places to be in front of viewers. The ad spend has moved to follow the audience.

ONLINE ALL THE TIME

Brands need to think digital first because their audience and customers already act that way. In the heyday of television advertising, a large effort was made to get audiences in front of the message. Now those eyeballs are increasingly on social media platforms. That's where attention and time is being spent, so that's where the money should be spent.

Advertising on television was traditionally controlled by broadcasting a limited number of TV channels. With social media, everyone is a potential broadcaster with the means and platform to publish work and ideas in multiple forms. The top earning Instagram influencers have engaged with people and developed their network, building communities. They are authorities in their niche. The messages on their feed command attention.

As audiences migrate to digital channels, a brand has various options within its digital media strategy to engage and promote the brand message. The obvious stalwarts of digital infrastructure are the website and, increasingly, smartphone applications which form the basis of a brand message. Since most people search online, you need to ensure your websites appear in search engine results organically through search engine optimization. Email marketing continues to be one of the strongest tools.[4] All of these marketing channels form the basis of traditional online digital marketing.

The innovation I see in digital marketing lies in the social aspect of digital. This covers content marketing including blogging, both organic and paid social media, and "influencer

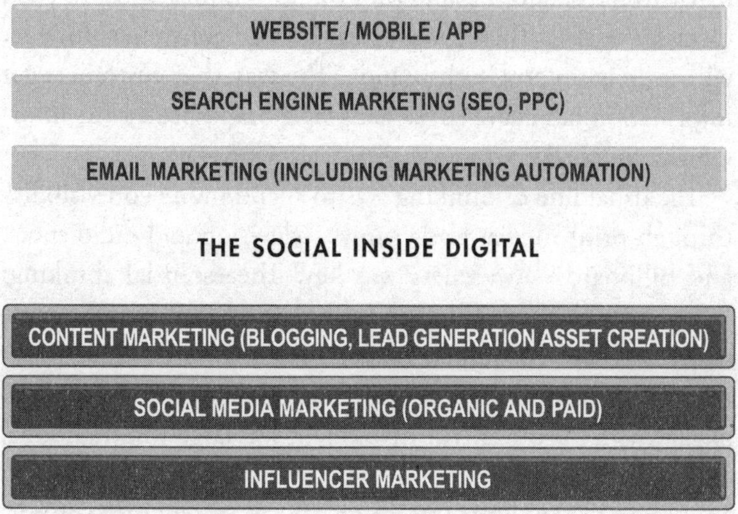

> **WEBSITE / MOBILE / APP**

> **SEARCH ENGINE MARKETING (SEO, PPC)**

> **EMAIL MARKETING (INCLUDING MARKETING AUTOMATION)**

THE SOCIAL INSIDE DIGITAL

> **CONTENT MARKETING (BLOGGING, LEAD GENERATION ASSET CREATION)**

> **SOCIAL MEDIA MARKETING (ORGANIC AND PAID)**

> **INFLUENCER MARKETING**

Figure 2.3

marketing" (see Figure 2.3). Influencer marketing is where you appeal to relationships on digital platforms, leveraging the social media presence of employees, fans, and influencers.

These three final aspects—content marketing, both paid and organic social media, and influencer marketing—are all heavily linked to social media. These are the biggest areas of innovation and of increased spending and growth.

THE DIGITAL TRANSFORMATION

There has been a fundamental shift in how we consume information, and how customers digest information.

Any essential guide to marketing teaches the Buyer's Journey: a linear model moving from awareness to consideration to purchase. It's a foundation to the entire perspective of what we try to do in marketing. The common approach through the twentieth century was to have as much control as possible over the first two steps, and the way your brand was presented, to push toward the sale. There's a shift in the way consumers interact with purchases and with brands. The way that customers get information has changed, so the way a brand broadcasts information must adapt, too.

The usual line of thinking was to spend money on visibility through print media, trade shows, television and radio spots, and billboards. Awareness was key. The essential thinking: Without visibility and buyer awareness of your brand's existence, how will consumers decide to buy your product? Back then there was no organic way outside of word of mouth to engage with the buyer. The investment was largely in traditional channels of communication because that's exactly where you could find the audience's attention. The more you spent on ads, the more eyeballs on your brand, the more your sales increased.

Today, audiences are on social and digital. So much information is user-generated that brands and companies don't have a monopoly on the information about themselves or their products. A potential buyer now does a Google search, reads a blog post, sees a social media post, asks on a forum and interacts with other prior customers. Buyers can learn what they need to know; you no longer get to tell them what they need to know.

It is widely quoted in marketing circles that over 50 percent of purchasing decisions are made before your business is contacted.[5] Customers have done their research, read reviews, and studied specifications. They are looking for the best product that suits their purpose. Even in a B2B environment, research is done online, with more than two-thirds of the buyer's journey done digitally according to Sirius Decisions.[6] Gone are the days of sole dependency on sales visits and presentations. How customers communicate with you is fundamentally different now. There is some control, but at the heart of it, the tables have turned. The power lies in consumers' ability to access a wealth of information, largely on the internet.

Brands shouldn't see this as losing control over how a message is positioned. Influencer marketing helps brands gain traction during the awareness and consideration steps in the changing digital landscape. Many have already adapted, extending the journey past the purchase into communication, like getting customers to leave a review of the product or share a picture of their food on Instagram.

THE RISE AND ROLE OF SOCIAL MEDIA

Social media plays a huge role in today's society. It's the top reason people use their laptops, tablets, and mobile devices. In the United States, five of the ten most visited websites are social media sites.[7] Audiences that used to be on television screens are on other screens now, often more than one at once.

Businesses can engage directly with customers on these social platforms and communicate with users through the role of content and influencers. This is the convergence of information and communication that social media represents.

These social sites were not made for businesses. They were created for people to communicate. In the case of Facebook, it was for college or high school friends to reconnect or stay in touch, for families to stay connected, or for people to connect with those around them. LinkedIn was for colleagues to communicate. SMS was initially utilized for notifications to mobile phones to inform users of voice mail messages. Now it's a major form of communication. People figure out how to use technology for their daily lives and end up hijacking it for utilitarian reasons. This is how technology evolves and will continue to do so.

The watershed moment in the evolution of social media happened in February 2009, when a U.S. Airways flight made an emergency landing on the Hudson River outside of New York City. People first learned about it on Twitter.[8] CNN covered it "as reported on Twitter." Now our newsfeeds are not just travel pictures and baby photos, it's where we find out what is happening in the world. Pew Research Center found that more than two-thirds of Americans get their news from social media (see Figure 2.4).[9]

The point is, social media is a legitimate source of news and information. If social media is about the convergence of information and communication, brands are at a distinct disadvantage simply because they can't communicate like people. A brand can't connect on the same level as a person. A company can't compliment someone's hairstyle. A product or app can't celebrate your team's win in the same way as another person.

PERCENTAGE OF US ADULTS WHO GET NEWS FROM SOCIAL MEDIA

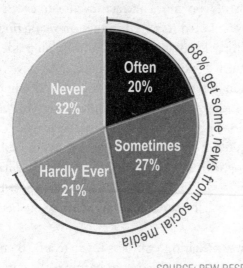

SOURCE: PEW RESEARCH CENTER

Figure 2.4

Some have tried by asking things like "how was your weekend?" It doesn't work as well as when a friend asks. Brands, therefore, need to play a different role in social media.

When asked about key factors when deciding on a purchase, consumers responded that they rely on trust and word of mouth well over 90 percent of the time.[10] The same survey showed that online reviews were trusted 70 percent of the time—essentially word of mouth in a digital world. It used to be that only certain sources could be so influential. People might rely on the opinion of a neighbor or friend, but it was those with publishing platforms who held real sway. Journalists, stock and financial analysts, athletes, and celebrities were the most common. In the B2B realm, buyers go through the same process. It's peer reviews, tech blogs, and opinions of others in the field that become the trusted source.

Take the example of a technology provider in the contact center industry who grew contract revenue in excess of 30 percent a year attributed to a B2B influencer marketing program. The company collaborated with an author, an academic, and a journalist-turned-blogger who blogged, hosted webinars, and had in-person events talking about issues important to the contact center industry. Another example is the VoIP and broadband solutions provider to small businesses who added more than $100,000 in new and additional recurring subscriptions by partnering with an entrepreneur-author and a small business growth expert who hosted multiple webinars and wrote several how-to guides that helped their audience make better buying decisions.[11]

In this new scenario, regardless if you're a B2B enterprise or a consumer-facing brand, content becomes the currency of social media for every company.

It is said that people buy from people and brands that they know, like, and trust. It's the role of content in social media that allows brands to be liked and to be able to create community, to be there and to respond, inspiring feelings of reliability, consistency, and trust.

While brands struggle to influence through content, influencers, who intrinsically are content creators, are masters at it. They present the trusted human voice and a personal relationship to other people on their network. This can be through reviews, conversations, blogs, podcasts, videos, photos, webchats, and all kinds of digital and social media communication. Brands have even started sourcing content from influencers, whose content is inherently engaging and authentic to the user experience. If content is now central to digital business communication, influencers will increasingly play a growing role as content creators.

SOCIAL MEDIA
WAS MADE FOR PEOPLE

The New Rules of Organic Social Media Marketing

Marketing strategy is about reaching your target audience. Social media strategy is an extension of that. Every time brands publish on social media, it's done with the hope that their content generates organic engagement, while building other benefits such as trust and stronger brand identity, moving potential customers down the marketing funnel.

However, brands have a distinct disadvantage in engagement on social media. The heart of this lies in the fact that social media was created for people, not for businesses. The social network algorithms that govern newsfeeds of social media users will always favor the content of people over businesses for a variety of reasons discussed later.

The challenge then is to leverage users whose content appears prominently in the newsfeeds of your target audience.

• • •

SOCIAL MEDIA TO SCALE

After the eventual growth of your social media community, the obvious tendency is to try to scale your marketing operations. Like other marketing channel strategies, when some success comes from a television or billboard campaign, perhaps a print ad campaign through magazines, the next step would be to push this further through scale to increase engagement and to generate a greater ROI. It stands to reason that brands will move to scale their social media presence with numbers of users growing and time spent inside social networks increasing.

The standard approach to scaling operations breaks down into three options:

People
Process
Tools

Scaling through one of these three options works on any marketing approach and they are relied on because they work . . . to an extent.

Increasing the breadth of your strategy and program by increasing manpower is a natural step. You can put more people on the project, increase the size of the team, look externally to outsource the work, or hire an agency to develop and scale the message for you. Scaling the manpower in this way can quickly raise the costs associated with labor. When you double the size of the community or number of conversations you have, do you double the size of your social media team? People can't scale, and therefore the return may not match the ratio of investment.

Tweaking your processes and optimizing what you do by pinpointing exactly where you can be more efficient is another common step. Looking at the processes by which you manage social listening, content creation, or social ad management might give you some ideas to slightly grow your organizational efficiency. Optimizing and targeting the message to your specific demographic cuts down on the waste or inefficient efforts. Trimming the fat is obviously efficient but might have limited positive impact on ROI.

Investing in tools, like ones discussed later, to refine, scale, or increase efficiency is another strategy tied to optimizing processes. Tools can provide analysis and insight as to how to optimize processes, increase efficiency, or where you might want to invest more or cut back. However, tools have their limitations as to the extent that they can help scale your social media program.

While increasing people, processes, and tools can aid the effectiveness of your social media program, this becomes difficult over time. The landscape for organic social media reach has drastically changed, and will continue to evolve in favor of people, not brands. When there is so much content being published around the clock, the supply and demand changes the playing field. More brands publish. More voices strain to be heard. More advertising is put into the world. But a user's newsfeed has limited space. People use social media to keep in touch with friends, not to see ads. Social networks must balance themselves on a tightrope of delivering content that people want to see with the minimum amount of advertising to satisfy their investors. With more and more messages vying for position, the return on these organic efforts in social media becomes increasingly limited.

THE HUMAN AND SOCIAL CONNECTIONS

A deeper understanding of how social media works is the first step in overcoming the challenges to organically building a brand. Often, it's less about the tools or the processes that can be wasteful, and more about understanding both the platform and the human connection that can help increase the efficiency of one's strategy. When you understand the social media platform and invest more in the human connection that makes social media so powerful, then you can tap into truly authentic organic engagement.

As a brand or business, it can be infuriating to establish your personality in social media marketing then find the playing field has changed. Embrace that the playing field will always be in flux. What's important is to understand the fundamental reason behind this changing landscape.

I had the privilege of visiting the Facebook campus at Menlo Park several years ago. As you drive out of the parking lot, every visitor and employee passes the old sign for Sun Microsystems. After several years of trouble, Sun Microsystems finally folded in 2009. Now the Facebook campus occupies its old building. The story goes that Mark Zuckerberg wanted to keep the sign up for a reason: If Facebook becomes irrelevant it will go the same way. Every employee is reminded of that fact as they leave the Facebook campus. Unless people engage with your content or your product, your company will go the same way as Atari, Borders, and Sun Microsystems. For Facebook, this means keeping people logging into their newsfeeds and engaging with the app or site. When people log out and step away, the company loses its audience. This is the reason Facebook strives to keep users engaged by changing the algorithm, minimizing exposure to obvious ads, and keeping interesting posts in the visible newsfeed. The newsfeed is the heart of any social network whose algorithm will determine its success or failure.

So, on top of the fact that a business can't effectively communicate in the same way people can, this changing algorithm affects your engagement, too.

For a brand or business to get its message to take root in this climate, it has to understand how to best use the Facebook feed. That means knowing how the algorithms work. This is not as easy as taking a peek under the hood. The algorithm is a closely guarded corporate secret, much like the Coca-Cola recipe or Google's own search algorithm. From information the company has released or spoken about publicly, we know that there are over 100,000 personalized factors dictating what each person sees and for how long.[1]

Based on my own experience and the opinions of experts in the space, we can simplify our understanding of any social media algorithm and approach organic content creation through the simplified formula in Figure 3.1.

In terms of *interest*, people will always outperform brands. We simply have greater affinity for loved ones than a loved brand. This immediately puts businesses at a disadvantage and

A SIMPLIFIED LOOK AT
SOCIAL MEDIA ALGORITHMS

CHANCES YOUR
POST IS SEEN BY = I x P x C x T x R
YOUR FANS

I — How engaged are you with the account?

P — How are others engaging with this post?

C — How have others engaged with this account's posts in the past?

T — Do users engage with this type of post?

R — How new is the post?

SOURCE: JOSH CONSTINE / TECHCRUNCH

Figure 3.1

explains why we see more posts by close family members than distant colleagues. If we "Liked" a business page some time ago, but never engaged with their content, we are telling the Facebook algorithm that we have no interest in them. This is why engagement becomes a tactic to help more of your fans see more of your content. The more fans engage with your content, the higher your *interest* score becomes with them.

Think of *post* in terms of a baseball batting average. If your post is released to a subset of fans in the newsfeed and performs well (people engage with it), then it will be shown to more fans. If it doesn't perform well, it won't be shown to any more fans.

The *creator* element: Think *post* score but over a longer time frame. If your published posts consistently bat high for engagement, Facebook thinks your content is engaging for your friends or fans and assumes more people will see future posts. The entirety of the engagement history with your social media account is used. Since people engage with people more than brands or businesses, this gives people, on average, a higher career batting average and a higher rate of their posts being seen.

As far as *type*, simple experimentation will show you that certain content media will perform better than others. For instance, for many brands, text posts perform worse than images or videos. Experimenting with this is core to finding ways to get your message across. Different types of messages and demographics react better to certain kinds of posts. This also changes over time as Facebook strategically tweaks their algorithm to favor certain types of content media over others.

Recency is self-explanatory. A new post will be seen more today than it will tomorrow unless it has somehow become more relevant, increased engagement, or gone viral.

All of this engagement data shapes the algorithm for each individual's newsfeed, across every social network.

ALCHEMY AND THE ALGORITHM

So how do you defeat the algorithm? How do you make the newsfeed work for you? How do you get your brand's message in front of more people?

First, experiment. Different things work for different companies and different demographics. Try different types of posts of varying content at different times of day. Each person is different—that's why Facebook considers 100,000 factors for each person's feed—and in a similar vein, each brand is different. How your fans interact with you is not the same as how they would interact with other brands. A brand like Coke is very visual and interacts with its followers differently than a brand like *The New Yorker*.

The second option: Beat the algorithm by paying for the privilege. Many marketers today already consider social media to be a pay-to-play game. I'm a big fan of paid social and have a policy within my own company that I don't take on clients unless they have a paid social budget.

In fact, paid social is so important that it becomes the fourth element in allowing you to scale your social media operations (see Figure 3.2).

Engaging with paid social lets you target and spread messages to your market as well as to places where you don't live or have a presence. I've found it's certainly helped me promote my message ahead of speaking appearances in places I don't have existing reach. For a conference speaking engagement, I can select the demographic and the location, target the message, and for a few dollars potentially reach a few hundred targeted people in a region where I have no previous exposure or audience. If social media is the amplifier, paid social is the accelerator.

I like to compare paid social to the water fountain. Whenever you are low on water—or your KPIs (key performance

SCALING YOUR SOCIAL

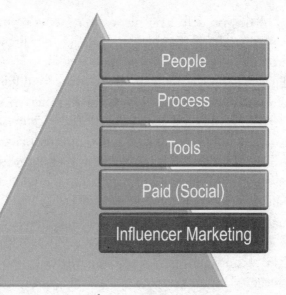

Figure 3.2

indicators) from organic social media are on the low side compared to your budget—you can immediately turn on the water with paid social and reach whatever marketing objectives you might have for your social media program. Paid social allows you to truly scale your social media marketing.

That brings us to the problems of paid social: It becomes more expensive with the increase in competition. Of the 350+ marketing teams and agencies that were asked in a recent *Relatable* "State of Influencer Marketing Report," seven out of ten agreed that Facebook Ads were getting increasingly expensive or harder to optimize.

On a social media network, paid social can still be seen as an advertisement in a world of organic user-generated content. For that reason, people might be hesitant or unlikely to engage with it. Some companies and brands are highly successful with this strategy and manage to get a lot of clicks and engagement. Other things, though they might tick all the boxes on paper, miss and strike out completely. It's far from being an exact science. We also know that consumers—and social media users— are becoming better and better at tuning out advertisements.

This has companies looking for other options. We now reach the fifth step in scaling your social media operations: influencer marketing, which leverages the power of people to communicate. If social media was made for people, and social network algorithms favor them, doesn't it make sense to make people an integral part of your social media strategy? Utilizing the voices of other users, companies have created programs to harness the power of social media users in three different ways:

Employee advocacy—where employees are leveraged

Brand advocacy—where fans are leveraged

Influencer marketing—where influential social media users are leveraged

Some see influencer marketing as a separate social strategy, but they are parts of the same pie and can be measured with the same KPIs. Whenever we collaborate with an individual who yields influence in a community we are trying to reach, whether that person's an outsider, a customer, or an employee, we are utilizing the same principles of influencer marketing.

Leveraging the power of people to help move your brand's needle forward is the common thread between each of these digital relationship marketing initiatives. Once you treat your employees and fans the same way you would influencers, you unlock the potential that all of these people have to spread your message in social media. That is why I will talk about employee advocacy and brand advocacy in later chapters.

Harnessing the potential of people power is the heart of influencer marketing. If people are spreading your message, then you sidestep the issue of being unable to interact on a personal level as a business. The issues that make social media engagement difficult as a brand are in many ways the same elements that make influencer marketing such a powerful resource. Everyone is a publisher. There are millions of voices in the social media ocean and newsfeeds are full of organic engagement. The best brand advocates speak in an authentic tone and are able to build much more trustful relationships than companies and brands.

Anyone can be an influencer now. Changing your social media strategy to engage with influencers taps into these voices and helps get around the disadvantage of being a brand and not a person.

Using tactically beneficial ways to help spread messages is nothing new in the history of modern communications. Consider its use by political demonstrations. The Tiananmen Square demonstrations in Beijing, China during the spring of 1989 saw the fax machine emerge as the communication tool of choice when the Chinese government restricted all other forms of communication. In a similar way, during the Occupy Wall Street movement when protesters populated the park, they were unable to run power to the site for amplification. When messages had to be spread to others listening, the speaker would say what they wanted to say and the people standing around that person would then repeat it, using ten voices to amplify the message and pass it on. This is people power and, in a much more analog way, the essence of what we do digitally on social media with influence marketing. We get those who have listeners and influence repeating the message.

We'll cover how to go about this later in the book. What's important to realize now is this doesn't end by throwing your message into the wind to hopefully drift down and land somewhere. Organic social media marketing involves tending to relationships to stimulate growth like most other elements involving the term *organic*.

Engaging in conversation and developing the human connection is essential. Social media sites are seeing the benefits of influencer engagement themselves. Platforms are finding they, too, can play a part in the new landscape and discovering that hosting influencer marketing on their platform is financially beneficial. Some, like Pinterest, might even see engaging with influencers as a way of staying relevant to marketers.

More tools now exist to measure and amplify. It's possible to bring more value to your investment and message through measuring and targeting. Facebook and Instagram now allow advertisers to track influencer posts and see how they're performing. When you can see the demographics reacting to the post, the type of post, and the level of engagement, you can improve its performance. It's also possible to boost these posts, spending your social media budget on boosting posts from influencers to reach more people and optimize ad spend. This all changes the playing field again. Once you understand the impact and potential of social media being made for people you begin to see the immense value that influencers can add to your business.

HOW VISUAL SOCIAL PRESENTS NEW CHALLENGES TO BUSINESSES AND NEW OPPORTUNITIES TO INFLUENCERS

The mainstream appeal of paid social for the modern marketer arises from the need to scale organic social media marketing and to overcome the bias against businesses inherent in social network algorithms. The recent rise of visual social, however, challenges the effectiveness of paid social in media where visual promotions look like blatant advertisements. These new challenges in visual social media have accelerated collaborations between brands and influencers.

THE RISE OF VISUAL SOCIAL

The rise of visual platforms and visual social media in recent years underscores another key reason influencer marketing is so important to helping brands reach their target audience. To be effective in communicating with customers—and the principle is the same whether a brand is customer-facing or B2B-oriented—

the brand must increasingly engage visually. Visual social has brought the importance of this to the forefront for all brands and industries.

Many newer social media platforms are predominantly visual. Older ones increasingly lean toward visual content. Facebook algorithms seem to favor the visibility of photos and natively uploaded videos, with images taking up more real estate in the newsfeed. Facebook emulated Instagram, which in turn was inspired by Snapchat, and also has its own Stories feature. A story can be told over multiple images with a twenty-four-hour time limit to induce more views. The live stream feature is becoming more popular. One might consider Instagram Stories to be a unique social network within its own network. Videos and images even fill the LinkedIn newsfeed, with livestreaming not far behind there as well. These new visual types of engagement unlock a range of ways to interact with social media users. The potential for businesses is huge, but not without pitfalls.

This sharp rise of visual social is best seen through the growth of Instagram, which rocketed into becoming the second-largest social network. Other rising networks reflect this visual component. Snapchat is almost entirely visual and 90 percent of users are between thirteen and twenty-four years old.[1] Pinterest has a smaller targeted demographic but in recent times generated the second-most social website traffic after Facebook—that is, traffic from social to sites outside social.[2] Pinterest pins and boards can also be found in Google searches, extending its value as a visual medium.

Visual posts are simply more engaging. They take up more space in the newsfeed of any given social network and are essential in communicating messages. The reason for this goes beyond any algorithm: It's biological. Humans receive more information from visual means than any other senses. Data shows 90 percent of information transmitted to the brain is visual.[3] On top of this, visual information is processed up to 60,000 times faster than text.

All of this means that you can communicate more with an image than with text, and in the case of social media it goes far beyond the old adage that a picture is worth a thousand words. A thousand words will still not engage in the same way that a properly managed visual face can connect with users. Engaging with visual language is key to communicate a message. Visual social media makes it essential.

THE STRUGGLE FOR A VISUAL VOICE

New types of visual communication have emerged so quickly that brands are still playing catch-up to align imagery from traditional advertising practices with visuals that are authentic and engaging to the average social media user. This process is the creation of a "visual voice." It is important that this voice doesn't make all the communication look like an advertisement.

Brands run into two major obstacles: developing a visual face or identity, then learning how to communicate through a visual voice. Not all brands or products translate well into a visual message. Engaging in a visual language is an art form, and not particularly natural. Companies who haven't engaged in print ads or TV ads are at a particular disadvantage. Many B2B brands find it even more challenging.

At the heart of their business, many brands are not visually inclined. Their products don't lend themselves to a particular visual identity or language, making the translation to a visual language more difficult. Those who succeed often approach the issue from another perspective.

One of my favorite innovative examples of how to engage in a visual language is from Maersk Line, which has actually won the award for "Social Media Campaign of the Year" at the European Digital Communication Awards, beating out both B2B and B2C competition.[4] As an industry-leading shipping company, it would be acceptable to assume that Maersk doesn't need to engage on a visual social level. But why not? Adding visual language only strengthens the brand and allows them to connect with and engage a huge global social media audience. Looking at their visual content, it's clear that they based their visual language on their global coverage. Having shipping containers worldwide reinforces the message the brand is trying to communicate. They also curated content on their social media platforms from users around the world, demonstrating that their reach truly was global.

This Maersk Line example answers questions that your brand might have about creating a visual voice. How do you engage with a visual voice when your company doesn't have one? When there's no image or human face to your company, does social media still work? Does a B2B company really benefit from engaging on visual social media?

Capitalizing on a visual identity and properly being able to communicate with a visual voice is an art form. For companies who haven't done print ads or TV ads where they've engaged with a visual message before, and particularly for many B2B companies, it can be more than a little challenging.

To see how your own brand and message can be put into visual language, you must delve into the language used by other brands. A visual audit of the Instagram feeds of companies who have a strong hold over their visual message is invaluable. Looking at competitors is a great place to start. I'll walk you through three companies with different approaches that reflect the identity of the product and brand in their own way. Note that this audit was done at a point in time reflected in the illustrations shown in the following figures, so these companies' most recent Instagram feeds probably will reflect an updated approach.

Sephora is a leading cosmetics retailer that's put a lot of thought into its visual voice. Their interesting display of color, contrasted with their iconic black and white theme, shows the heart of the message behind the makeup they sell. The contrast with textures, the inclusion of food and other elements the same color as the makeup—like cookies and ice cream—along with the way makeup colors are displayed makes it stand out. It gives Sephora their own strong visual voice. It's a creative way to show the product. The Instagram feed is scattered with some examples of their makeup on faces as well as reposts from influencers of other brands with whom they market (see Figure 4.1). A lot of this content is curated and reposted rather than created by the company. There are posts of faces wearing makeup in the way

SEPHORA'S INSTAGRAM FEED

Figure 4.1

you would expect from a cosmetics company, but many of the images show it in less traditional ways. In fact, the content, that we can assume was created by the brand itself, is the creative showcase of their colors and mashups of textures and elements.

In the case of the high-end American department store Nordstrom, we see that they sometimes actually cut off the faces of the models in their images (see Figure 4.2). The focus is clearly on the product. Despite being a store that sells a range of products covering all kinds of fashion and home furnishings, their visual social media as depicted on Instagram deals only with women's fashion. There's no men's fashion on display in their visual media. They're not trying to convey everything with their social media, but more a specific audience they want to talk to visually that they have defined as their target audience on Instagram.

NORDSTROM'S INSTAGRAM FEED

Figure 4.2

Target solved their visual language issues and the obstacle of preventing their visual social from looking like advertisements by removing people completely and infusing creativity into their content (see Figure 4.3). They used bright colors and arranged items from their stores in unlikely ways. A backpack becomes a face laughing at us. Even words, like "free shipping," are displayed written in packing tape, another product sold at Target stores. The images are sparse, product-centric, and creative, adding a playfulness and humor to the visual work instead of a sales-minded approach.

All three of these examples show companies with defined visual voices specific and well developed to the brand. They convey the brand's attitudes, engage creatively and playfully, or in other ways reflect the brand's culture. This is the challenge. This is why it's so hard for brands to present themselves on visual social.

TARGET'S INSTAGRAM FEED

Figure 4.3

In fact, more and more brands are deciding to not even attempt to present themselves on visual social and literally let their fans do the talking for them. This is exactly what The Walt Disney Company did to promote their parks.[5] While Disneyland has a large number of images to draw on from their decades of films and the history of their theme parks, when engaging with Instagram users, Disneyland relies on curating the content of Instagram users to engage with fan-produced images from within the parks. Stepping away from a professional look is a bold step, particularly for an already very visual brand that famously controls its image, but this approach captures the essence of what the brand wants to represent on their social networks—people exploring and enjoying the happiest place on earth.

WHAT IS AN AD?

There is often a gap between the social media visuals companies publish and the visuals consumed by users. If you're operating a large company, you might have noticed discrepancies between the material developed and promoted by your traditional marketing division and your newer social media team. Both begin differently with different goals.

Take an Instagram feed for example. You'll often see a clear distinction between what is and isn't an advertisement. Many companies are still treating social media as a forum and vehicle for advertisement. Social media is fundamentally different, and your social media audience generally does not react well to advertisements in their newsfeeds. Social media is not a place for a billboard or television community. It's a forum where people can engage with content. By treating social media like you would other media, you miss the potential for audience engagement.

This is where influencers come into play. Influencers are able to present visual messages more easily than brands. Today's influencers are often fluent at speaking a visual language. They already know what works. They connect with people because they are people. The influencer is not constrained by the limitations of a brand.

Visual messaging is hard. Content curation is the easiest way to tap into influencers, who can bring the power of visual language to your brand. Influencers already speak a visual language and show experience speaking that language, with a strong track record of engagement with their followers. That's exactly why you see a lot of influencer marketing initiatives on these newer visual platforms.

Forming the visual identity, engaging in storytelling, then dealing with a network you can't figure out can be baffling. This presents another kind of influencer marketing strategy which will be covered in more detail later: the account takeover. This would have been unheard of in the past, but now it's a strategy that has been implemented by many. Brands who want to connect with a demographic give the control of their account, often on a visual heavy platform, to an influencer who knows the platform and speaks to the demographic the brand wants to reach. The account takeover often lasts for twenty-four hours but some brands have done so for as long as a week. It presents an interesting angle to engage with influencers and reach users.

Confectionary brand Sour Patch Kids identified Snapchat as being essential to tap into their target demographic. Realizing that the rules for Snapchat were different, they reached out to a leading influencer in that demographic, Logan Paul. The brand gave Paul free rein over their Snapchat account, allowing him to produce content and interact with his audience and followers through their accounts. The weeklong campaign returned 120,000 new Snapchat followers, 6.8 million Snapchat impressions, and more than 26,000 screenshots.[6]

LEVERAGING VISUAL INFLUENCE

At a marketing conference in Las Vegas, I moderated a panel at which a marketing executive for one of the leading local hotel brands talked about often being approached by influencers who offered to tweet or Instagram their stay at the hotel in return for complimentary nights or products. This is a common strategy for hotels and influencers, so common that some hotels now no longer work with influencers in this manner because of the sheer numbers of inquiries they receive from people who might not be as influential as they claim.[7]

This hotel went the opposite direction by realizing that influencers can communicate better visually and that's the value they bring to the hotel. Now this hotel only engages with influencers when the influencer can provide a certain number of photos, a certain number of videos, and sign off on the use of the images so the hotel can use them in their organic marketing as well as advertising, not just the influencer's social media feed. By managing the interaction and transaction this way, the hotel taps into the power of the visual message through leveraging the user-generated content of content creators. It helps create an aligned visual voice and provides greater ROI through acquisition of a reusable asset created by an expert in the field. It is another type of ROI that can be derived from working with influencers and can have a longer-lasting impact than a traditional short-term marketing campaign. In fact, many brands now want to engage with influencers not necessarily for their content amplification but to tap into their content creation and use it to augment or even replace internally created visual assets.

ALL BAR ONE

ALL BAR ONE IS A LEADING CHAIN OF UK BARS and restaurants famous for an extensive cocktail menu. To bring more attention to a new summer menu, particularly the brunch options, All Bar One worked with Takumi (https://takumi.com), an influencer marketing company, to engage influencers. The brand focused on female millennials.

The bar engaged ten female micro-influencers with a high number of followers in the appropriate demographics to each post ten images of themselves enjoying brunch at one of the restaurants. Identifying the influencers was the first step. It was essential that the influencers had some pull in the realm of food and lifestyle and an authentic voice. The brand looked for a high percentage of engagement as a micro-influencer, rather than a larger following. The brand also included the rights to the images in the terms of engagement, meaning that All Bar One could reuse the images in their campaigns.

The images were shared on the bar's and influencers' Instagram channels using #brunchie. The posts were supported by a social media advertising angle, and a competition to encourage other diners to share their own #brunchie photos for a chance to win a Mulberry Kite handbag. This extra engagement brought the hashtag to everyday patrons, strengthening the brand's identity and pull in general, not just in brunch dining.

The campaign ran for a month, during which the restaurants reported a 28 percent customer increase. On social media, however, All Bar One experienced nearly a 600 percent rise in engagement on Instagram with the use of hashtags including #brunchie and #brunch, and a 60 percent increase on other networks. The campaign generated a reach of 177,228 people with 5,931 likes and 114 comments. That equated to an overall engagement rate of 4.9 percent.

Influencers bring an authenticity and human touch to a brand message that brands can't deliver on their own.

Chinese airline Xiamen Air engaged with influencers to spread the message that travelers could now fly nonstop from North America to China and use Xiamen as a base to fly all over Asia. One particular image represented an influencer's voice as a mother and family woman. The image of her gorgeously dressed toddler sitting on a large and decorated bed holding a model Xiamen Air model plane and explaining how they hope to take their daughter to places like Bali in the future is an image and story that the airline itself couldn't have created authentically (see Figure 4.4). It humanized the brand, engendered

PEOPLE TELL STORIES THAT BRANDS CAN'T

bubbly.and.blush • Follow

bubbly.and.blush Before we had Aleia hubby & I enjoyed traveling & one of our fave places to go to is Bali. We can't wait to be able to bring Aleia there to experience the beautiful Balinese culture! Xiamen Airlines a member of the SkyTeam Alliance has routes available from LA, NY, Seattle & Vancouver to Bali & so many beautiful countries!! We look forward to traveling more as a family & flying with a reputable airline!   [ad] #FlyForBetterWorld #XiamenAirlines @xiamenairlines

#girlmom #toddlerstyle #lovelylittlesquares #toddlersofig #mynameismama #documentyourdays #momlifeisthebestlife

1,133 likes

FEBRUARY 27

Figure 4.4

immediate authenticity, and gave the brand image an emotional quality. A paid promotion of their own photo, even the same photo, wouldn't have had the same impact as the influencer's posted image.

Visual social has proven to be a powerful accelerator in brands creating relationships with influencers, but also in their deriving greater ROI from those relationships. It is another reason, similar to social network algorithms favoring people, why engaging with influencers solves a business problem that is challenging for brands to overcome.

YOUR COMMUNITY
IS ALWAYS A SUBSET

The power of influencer marketing comes down to engaging your community. A brand's community of customers and followers is always a small subset of its potential in any given industry. In other words, people who already know you already know you: The value in influencer marketing through social networking comes from tapping into those who don't fully know or understand the value of your brand. This is where influencers can elevate a brand in the sea of billions of users represented by social media.

Just as there are different approaches with a short-term marketing campaign for quicker results and marketing strategy for a longer term return, there are influencer campaigns and influencer marketing. A long-term view must be taken to get the most out of influencer marketing. Using short-term campaigns brings smaller returns, often at a higher cost, but the true power of influencer marketing comes in taking a longer term approach.

Longer term influencer marketing is about community, not a campaign. That's a main point I try to drive home to clients and when I speak at conferences. Undertaking a traditional marketing campaign with specific KPIs and ROI measurement might be familiar ground for you, but the returns will be shorter term and largely confined to the time frame you choose to run the campaign.

Influencer marketing has a longer tail that involves more investment—in time and in other ways I'll address in later chapters—than running a traditional marketing campaign. It also brings more returns because of how it engages with people.

This concept of community over campaign is an undeniable key to engaging with people and underlies a fundamental mind-set shift. Building a community is a longer-lasting way to gather people around your brand or product. Once you've established a community, any campaign you launch has a foundation to start with and a cumulative effect to follow. Digital interactions have completely changed the ability to build a community.

A BRAND IN THE OCEAN

As a brand in the ocean of social media, you have a singular, lonely presence among hundreds of millions of users. Facebook and Instagram each have over a billion users. Other social networks like Twitter and LinkedIn have hundreds of millions of users. Those numbers dwarf your one voice. Influencer marketing is about harnessing the numbers in your favor.

As mentioned earlier, all companies begin with an organic presence. Building the community is just the very first part of the work. Initially your message spreads as your community grows and you develop your brand's social media strategy and online presence. Due to declining reach from the way that so-cial network newsfeed algorithms work, social media marketing becomes a pay-to-play initiative.

The essential truth is this: The community you've built, even after all the work you've put in through both organic and paid means, is only a small subset of the potential community that exists in social. Your brand's message has only spread so far. Unless you're the King Kong of the marketplace you'll see many competitors with a bigger share than yourself. Of course, you've been comparing yourself to competitors for the whole plan. The larger truth is that your competitor is also only taking ad-vantage of a subset of its potential as well.

Like most things, taking the first step is acceptance. In order to take the next step in spreading your message, you must first accept that no matter how big your community is, you've only tapped into a small percentage of what it could be.

The second step is seeing the data. Facebook Ads Manager can give insight into the figures of the potential audience. Re-gardless of your own community, fans, and followers, Facebook will show you that there is a greater number of people who have an interest in what you're selling. These figures come from Face-book users interacting with various Facebook pages, discus-sions, groups, and content, so we can reasonably assume that it's an accurate figure backed by data. As specific as your search and filters are—and the more specific to your demographic, the better informed you'll be—you will find a wide gulf between the community you have engaged and the number of people with an interest.

This is the delta in potential user engagement. Let's look at some specific examples to better understand this concept.

• • •

DEFINING THE DELTA

Let's consider a company that manufactures dark hair color. After they develop their community and spread their message through the usual social campaigns, it will become clear that their community is only a subset of the available market.

Using Facebook Ads Manager, we see that there are more than 37 million people with some interest in hair color. When I filter this by selecting only those in the United States, this number falls to 14 million.

Next, we analyze the size of American Facebook fans in the Facebook Ads Manager for the following leading hair color brands:

Clairol (Proctor & Gamble): 760,000
Dark and Lovely (L'Oréal): 110,000
Creme of Nature (Revlon): 74,000

We can see the gap that all of the leading brands have in terms of their current fan base and the potentially larger community they might be able to obtain. Even the leading brand, Proctor & Gamble, has less than 6 percent of the potential community! Until Clairol has engaged all 14 million people interested in hair color in the selected demographic, it is missing its potential reach. This is the delta of potential user engagement.

There might be other things to consider behind these numbers. It's possible these brands don't serve the entire demographic. It's possible there are sectors of the 14 million member community that these brands overlook. These missing community members might include men, while the brands are geared specifically toward female hair color enthusiasts. Or the brand is only geared toward people with naturally dark hair colors. Narrowing the demographic is important to consider and can help later when targeting the delta for your own community engagement. Regardless, it's not hard to recognize that even the largest brands have a community size that's a subset of the potential 14 million hair color fans.

Let's look at the car rental market, where the interest in the United States, according to the Facebook Ads Manager, is 8.4 million people. For the leading U.S. car rental companies with accessible data, we see the following Facebook fan numbers:

Hertz: 890,000
Enterprise: 210,000
National: 150,000

Hertz, the rental company with the largest number of Facebook fans, engages with only about 10 percent of the potential market (see Figure 5.1). Even considering demographic and

YOUR COMMUNITY IS ALWAYS A SUBSET

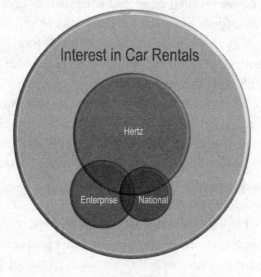

Figure 5.1

geographical limitations, the potential for growth in the delta is huge.

CONNECTING THE DELTA

We've put the delta into terms of numbers. But how do you connect with that other part of the market? How do you bridge the delta?

One strategy is to simply amplify your message through paid social. However, you would incur an astronomical cost and effort to reach those people. Bridging the delta of potential user engagement with a paid social campaign brings no guarantee that those who have never engaged with your brand before will engage now through these ads. Running this strategy does not promise engagement.

Paid social is still an advertisement. Social media users who have no affinity for your brand might be exposed to your brand's presence through an ad, but whether they decide to join your community or interact with your content will depend on a number of factors. Obviously, the greater affinity a particular user has for your brand, the greater the chance that they will interact with your advertisement.

Paid social at times is a viable option, but to capitalize on your message it's essential to think about community, not a campaign. At this point, you've already built a community, and you can leverage those fans you already have to expand your message and grow your community.

Enter influencer marketing.

One goal of influencer marketing is to leverage your community to spread the message for you. Another goal is to tap into leaders in the community who will assist in promoting you to their followers. It's about having others talk about your brand

and develop your community through word of mouth. It's utilizing the democratization of authority and other communities to bring more people to your message. By tapping into an influencer and the trust of her fans, you have the ability to expand your market reach in social media via more organic ways.

This is a universal concept that equally applies to B2C brands and B2B companies and even extends to nonprofit organizations. There is no brand or company that cannot benefit from tapping into the power of influencers in their particular industry.

ENGAGING HUMAN TRUST

It comes down to two core facts: People trust people more than ads, and social media was created for people, not businesses.[1] Viral campaigns, including incredibly successful ones such as the Ice Bucket Challenge, spread through the organic engagement in social media presenting a short-term growth. You can harness that power of social media with influencer marketing, turning it into community.

Paid social has its limitations. But if someone with influence over a particular community says something great about your brand, or even just exposes you to their community, you'll see a visible ROI of users engaging with you. We'll cover the intangible benefits of developing community and organic engagement in the following chapters.

Tapping into the trust that social media users place in other people and people of authority like influencers will help your brand get positive exposure, and spread your message, and reach a larger percentage of that vast delta of potential engagement.

PART TWO

UNDERSTANDING INFLUENCERS AND THE WAYS YOU CAN ENGAGE WITH THEM

The rise of social media and the development of our online personalities mean everyone has some online presence. An influencer is anyone with an audience and a platform, who has weight with their followers. Chances are you're in touch with influencers more than you realize. The key to leveraging their influence is finding who fits with your message.

One question that often arises: "Why would an influencer want to work with me?" Mutual benefit. The influencer gets something from you, too. And it's not always money. Selecting the right influencer is important. There's a way to find out if what you and the influencer want are the same thing, and how you can work together to achieve goals for both of you.

Working with an influencer isn't a one-time deal. As I like to put it: Influencer marketing is a marriage, not a one-night stand. A one-time campaign can bring quick results but the true power of engaging with an influencer, and the large-scale return, comes when you develop a relationship.

UNDERSTANDING THE INFLUENCER LANDSCAPE

The Different Types and Levels of Influencers

The definition of an influencer is as broad as the definition of influence. By taking a look at the different types and levels of influencers, you will begin to better picture those influencers who will best fit your company's plans.

When we talk about the kinds of influencers we can work with and how they fit with the entire social media landscape, we have to remember why influencers exist in the first place. People make decisions based on advice from people they trust. Increasingly, though, we are influenced by people we don't know personally but have gotten to know through social media.

Beyond this, people want to hear from trusted voices with authority. Traditionally speaking, the trusted sources were businesses and the media. There were—and still are—entire departments within companies responsible for media relations, ensuring brand messages were released to the appropriate people. Brands had spokespeople to make statements to people with influence who would then broadcast the message to their viewers, listeners, or readers. This is essentially pre-social media content sharing through the "clips" of press releases.

The core reason companies and brands wanted these voices remains the same in the social media world: People trust people.

Influencers influence because they produce content that is heard, listened to, and trusted. Whether it's a TV show or a financial market column, a blog post or a YouTube channel, this is trusted content. Anyone can be a publisher these days, and anyone can be an influencer, including family and friends, peers and practitioners. Whether it's Yelp reviews, blogs, podcasts, photos, social conversations, tweets, LinkedIn posts, YouTube videos, or an Instagram image, everyone is producing content for an audience that's spending more time on social media.

INFLUENCER AUDIENCE CLASSIFICATION

Let's start by separating influencers into manageable classifications. I will look at two ways of approaching this. The size of a given influencer's followers or community is one approach. We can classify influencers into five groups based on size of audience (see Figure 6.1). Note that the number of followers is only an estimated way of segmenting users, not an exact science, but these are tiers commonly used when filtering influencers on Instagram.

The **Celebrity** category is made up of the largest audiences, the social media accounts with over a million followers. Many of these are public figures already. They have developed their audience and built their own online brand. It's important to remember that public figures or celebrities are not always influencers when it comes to social media. Someone who has a high visibility but doesn't translate to a social media presence is not an influencer. Unless they shift their audience to a social media

THE TIERS OF
INFLUENCE ON INSTAGRAM

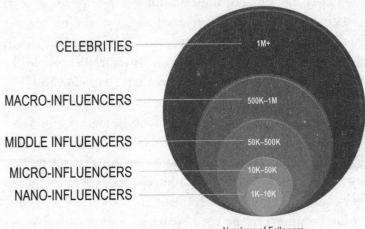

CELEBRITIES —————————————— 1M+

MACRO-INFLUENCERS ————————— 500K–1M

MIDDLE INFLUENCERS ————————— 50K–500K

MICRO-INFLUENCERS ————————— 10K–50K

NANO-INFLUENCERS ————————— 1K–10K

Numbers of Followers

SOURCE: MEDIAKIX

Figure 6.1

setting, their place as a trusted voice doesn't translate within the realm of social media. Singers and musicians such as Beyoncé, Selena Gomez, and Taylor Swift are all prominent on Instagram. Others like Bono from U2 or Coldplay front man Chris Martin are certainly comparable celebrities but haven't transferred their audience into an equally influential social media presence. Although Coldplay has an Instagram account, Chris Martin doesn't engage personally.

Retired Los Angeles Lakers' star Kobe Bryant is an example of an athlete who achieved celebrity status. After initially not engaging on social media and actually stating that he didn't see the point, Bryant now has a following in the millions on Instagram. Bryant built his online brand. He is famously ambitious and aspirational and perhaps this swayed his thinking about social media engagement. Following his retirement, Bryant has continued to engage his social media audience as he builds his own brands in sportswear and entertainment.

A new generation of nontraditional celebrity influencers have emerged who have leveraged social media to become equally influential. These are people older generations might not know but younger generations do. This includes people like the YouTuber Logan Paul, with more than 10 million YouTube subscribers, and Kayla Itsines, "the most influential fitness star in the world" with more than 10 million Instagram followers.[1] Daniel Middleton, the British YouTuber who is also the world's highest paid YouTube star, began by creating Minecraft reviews.[2] These are all celebrities within the realm of social media: They could not have become influencers without social media.

Macro-influencers are the next largest group, with follower counts numbering from half a million to a million. They influence on a large scale and might elevate into becoming a celebrity of their own over time. Macro-influencers have a large enough audience size to guarantee a significant amount of engagement for any brand that works with them.

Middle influencers comprises the group with audiences ranging from fifty thousand to half a million. At this level of influence, the influencer is beginning to charge more for posts and engagement. They often know the power of their community and are actively building it. Until recently, this level of influence had often been the lowest that many companies would approach. This view is understandable but overlooks the potential of engagement with smaller communities.

Micro-influencers are those with ten thousand to fifty thousand followers who are increasingly popular to work with because of the authenticity and "nicheness" of their communities. The sheer numbers of micro-influencers online make them an increasingly popular entity to engage with. One report stated that a total of 84 percent of sponsored posts on Instagram came from this demographic.[3] Some platforms that work with connecting influencers with brands will only work with those whose audiences number over ten thousand. For this reason, many see this as the lowest level of influencer, discounting any audience lower than this.

Nano-influencers, those with an audience of one thousand to ten thousand, are often overlooked but are gaining in popularity for the same reasons micro-influencers are. I certainly think they have their place and should be recognized, especially in niche industries. Despite their small audiences, they are often well-connected and better able to communicate on a personal level with their communities. As we know, followers can be bought, and the numbers can be manipulated. Working with a nano-influencer who has a strong level of engagement is likely to give better returns than an influencer with ten thousand followers but a weak community.

HISMILE

MANY START-UPS NOW ENGAGE DIRECTLY WITH their target demographic through social media, opting to bypass traditional advertising as a first step. How can influencers help you break into your market? Can using only influencers help you grow in the traditional business sense?

HiSmile was started by two friends on the Gold Coast of Australia, intent on creating an easy-to-use teeth-whitening product.[4] From the beginning, HiSmile saw the strength in engaging with influencers. Their first step was making sure they had a product they were confident in and able to present to influencers. They approached influencers and gifted products hoping for mention in social feeds. They focused heavily on smaller and micro-influencers with a strong following in certain regions. After months of experimenting, HiSmile found millennial women were their biggest market. They adjusted their program to reflect this.

The influencer program grew and after several years, Hi-Smile's pool of influencers numbered over two thousand. Through experimentation, the brand learned that Instagram was the best performing social media network but still spent time tapping into other networks. Facebook presents a large share of the HiSmile influencer campaign, followed by You-Tube and Twitter. Snapchat didn't provide the results that HiSmile was looking for and so they scaled back their efforts there, though still kept a presence.

HiSmile reposts and shares their influencers' content and continues to engage in their conversations. The constant commenting keeps a fresh and personal approach to the brand's own account and continues the engagement with influencers beyond the product posts. They also engage with potential clients, answering questions and reposting results from their teeth-whitening products. The HiSmile feed also includes a great deal of comedy targeted at the fashion-conscious millennial audience.

After several years of positive results, HiSmile decided to invest in influencer marketing on a larger scale. They approached celebrities including Kylie Jenner and Conor Mc-Gregor. Of course, engaging with a celebrity influencer involved an investment beyond product gifting. Working with McGregor was a strategic move to connect with the male millennial market, with the hope of recreating their success with female millennials. The brand continues to invest in social media influencers with a high level of success.

SIZE DOESN'T (ALWAYS) MATTER

Influencer size doesn't always matter. In fact, many large audiences are not engaged at the rate of smaller audiences. Studies have shown that for Instagram audiences, the percentage of likes as a percentage of followers peaks around a thousand followers with 8 percent engagement (see Figure 6.2).[5] As the audience grows to over a million followers, the engagement declines to 2 percent of the community. The highest rate of engagement is seen for the nano-influencer category (under 10,000 followers) with about 6 percent engagement.

Smaller influencers are listened to and valuable. Sometimes a deeper, more personal connection can be developed with a nano-influencer than someone with a million followers. These smaller influencers can have more sway with their communities; from the perspective of a brand hoping to engage with this community, they are easier to succinctly target and reach. By

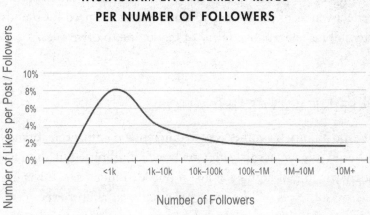

**INSTAGRAM ENGAGEMENT RATES
PER NUMBER OF FOLLOWERS**

SOURCE: MARKERLY

Figure 6.2

looking at the number of engagements one might expect to receive based on past performance as opposed to pure follower count, you have the potential to re-evaluate those with smaller communities and see how they might generate greater ROI compared to influencers with a much larger community size but with much less engagement.

Recent research shows celebrities, despite their glamorous appeal, are not always the greatest influencers. A study from Collective Bias showed 70 percent of millennials are more likely to listen to a non-celebrity influencer, further highlighting the importance of smaller influencer potential.[6] The same study showed only 3 percent of people would consider buying a product in-store if it was endorsed by a celebrity. The study showed that a growing percentage of the global population has a completely different "digital native" perspective on celebrities and influence. Celebrity testimonials, together with traditional advertising vehicles such as TV and print advertisements, measured as the least-influential forms of communication when shopping for products in-store. It is a reminder of the declining effectiveness of traditional advertising and the need for brands to embrace alternative forms of marketing to drive sales.

AFFINITY CLASSIFICATION

Brand affinity is another way to differentiate influencers. Brands should engage across different levels of affinity, but the tendency is to look immediately for outside influencers. Engaging across all levels will be more productive in almost every case. This approach, to go outside first, carries over from thinking in terms of traditional approaches to marketing: The best amplification is outside the company, someone with an outsized voice like a celebrity spokesperson or industry analyst. In influencer marketing, it's the opposite. Since everyone is a publisher and everyone is an influencer, engaging those with an affinity for your brand already is a much stronger first step.

The first level of the affinity search is employees (see Figure 6.3). This is such an important and overlooked aspect of engagement. The livelihood of your employees is directly tied to the success of your brand, so it's only natural that they become your most passionate advocates. Now that social media is truly a mainstream communication channel transcending generations, it's safe to say an overwhelming majority of today's employees have their own social presence, place on networks, and way of sharing information. When there's a major accomplishment for the brand, or a new product they're proud to be involved with, it makes sense to encourage employees to share the information with their audience. Capitalizing on your employees' own networks brings huge benefits and not just in promoting your brand—employee engagement is a wonderful side-effect of utilizing this tactic properly.

INFLUENCER AFFINITY CLASSIFICATION

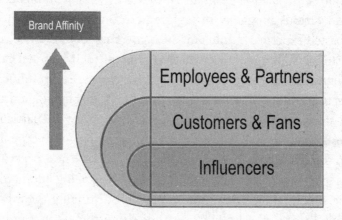

Figure 6.3

However, there are many aspects to consider before engaging with your employees over social media. It's not about having them promote a sale or the fact your company is offering free shipping over the weekend. Your employees don't want to spam their friends with your promotions. It is about engagement, forming a collaborative relationship for leverage. Establishing a mutually beneficial employee advocacy program is the first step.

Fans and brand advocates are the next level of affinity engagement. These people are already your customers. They like your product, are engaged with your brand, and want to share information about your company. They have a vested interest as a consumer. In a B2B setting they're often customers who like and use your product, resellers/distributors, or ecosystem partners. Identifying the voices of influence among your fans and how they can engage with their communities provides you with a powerful relationship you can leverage. Turning your fans into true brand advocates takes commitment from the brand. You want to make the fans feel special.

One example of the power of brand advocates is Dutch supermarket chain Albert Heijn, who developed a long-term brand ambassador program engaging fifty-eight influencers.[7] The various bloggers, Instagrammers, and other influencers boasted expertise in different areas covering food, lifestyle, and fashion. When looking to activate one of their seasonal campaigns, Albert Heijn would engage the relevant expert influencers to promote their message or amplify it, through digital and in-store initiatives. The brand worked to ensure the particular posts were aligned with their marketing campaigns to capitalize on the reinforced message on social networks. These expert influencers took part in sixteen campaigns engaging and netting the supermarket 23 million impressions, bringing them both digitally and physically closer to their customers in a unique and authentic way.

Establishing a brand advocacy program is a fine first step and allows you to begin the conversation about what kind of rewards your fans would enjoy. Some approaches work better than others, depending on the type of product and brand. A discount code could work well for a company engaged in software development, whereas a sportswear company might find their fans react better to free merchandise. It's a conversation you have to start in order to find out what works for your fans. Having this conversation with your fans also gives you a good idea about how to reach out to the third level of affinity influencers—those outside the affinity circle.

Brands often look for outside influencers first. The first step should be the opposite. The best connections are the ones you have already. Engage within the circle of affinity, then look to outside influencers, then people with larger audiences with whom you want to connect. Finding and engaging those outside influencers through paid methods or advocacy or affiliate programs is harder. You already have a relationship with employees and fans.

IT'S A MARRIAGE, NOT A ONE-NIGHT STAND

Influencer marketing is about creating a long-term community, not about launching a one-off campaign. When you engage employees or fans, you're working within the community already around your brand. When approaching outsiders, it's important to remember that influencer marketing is about community, not a campaign.

It's not a one-night stand. Seek a long-term commitment when engaging potential influencers if you want to have the best chance of converting them into brand advocates, where your brand name might become a natural part of their online vocabulary. Initially, you need to find the influencers who are right for you. Employees and fans have, to some degree, chosen you. How you engage them is a conversation you have to have to make the relationship work. Why would your employee want to spread your news on their personal network?

You're asking an influencer to bring their community to you when you approach them to spread your message. Sometimes the information spread is not as important as who spreads it. Everyone is a content creator, and some influencers are content amplifiers as well. In fact, many are *just* amplifiers. There are some very large and influential Instagram channels that only repost other people's photos each day. Having your own photo or content amplified on these channels brings you to the attention of the community around this influencer.

Just as it's difficult for a brand to engage on social media in the same way that a person can, it's difficult for a brand to connect to a potential influencer on a human level. Overcoming this obstacle has been hard for brands for decades. It is why companies had spokespeople or press relations departments. Now the power lies in creating a human connection to those with sway on social media who hold a voice of trust.

LACROIX

BRAND AFFINITY IS DIFFICULT TO CREATE. IT stands to reason that engaging with your fans first can be a powerful step. That's what sparkling water brand LaCroix has focused on in recent years. In a market where the giants are produced by Nestlé and Pepsi, LaCroix engaged with fans and social media instead of traditional marketing avenues such as television commercials.

LaCroix focuses its attention on micro-influencers in the key millennial demographic.[8] The brand's values resonate with the ideas of authenticity, exploration, and fitness often sought by these users. The brand encourages its fans to post content using hashtags like #LaCroixLove and #LiveLaCroix. LaCroix's own social media channels are used to distribute cocktail and mocktail recipes. They also share curated recipes from fans.

Engaging directly with fans, the brand reposts content from users with as few as 150 followers, opting for community and key values over high-visibility influencers. Engaging with fans for being fans taps into authentic voices and makes sure the fans know they're listened to and appreciated. The brand has also attached itself to clean eating and fitness campaigns, finding extra traction aligning with trends such as Whole30, a month-long clean eating program.

All this engagement showed results on Instagram, the platform focused on by the brand, helping LaCroix grow its community from 4,000 to 30,000 in eight months. Aided in part by online engagement, sales doubled over two years to $225.5 million, making LaCroix second in the market to Nestlé.

INFLUENCERS AND THE LONG TAIL

Although the concept has been around since the 1940s, the *long tail* has gained increased popularity in the business and marketing field since Chris Anderson's article in *Wired* in 2004 (see Figure 6.4).[9] Anderson argued that the future of business, and the model that Amazon and Apple (among many others) used, was based on selling less for longer.

The initial fever in which the next *Star Wars* film is released on DVD means stores will stock and shelve many units for the

THE LONG TAIL

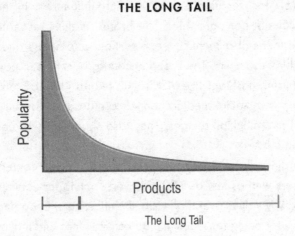

SOURCE: CHRIS ANDERSON / WIRED

Figure 6.4

release. The second week will not sell as many as the first week, and in the fourth week it will sell less than the third week. By the third month, daily sales will be significantly lower. Stocking DVDs takes space and the rate of sale will at some point be too low for the store to stock the DVD in the same numbers—if at all. People may still want to buy the DVD a year later but not in enough numbers to be in the store's best interest to stock the DVD. This is the reality facing physical stores with limited shelving space. This benefits companies like Amazon who can cater to this concept of selling more for longer. They capitalize on the long tail. They can stock books and movies, for example, that people will engage with long after the fever of the initial release.

When applied to marketing, the idea translates to a campaign with a shelf life that's often short. After weeks, if not months, of preparation you launch your campaign. You post videos and launch hashtags, wanting to see the new product or campaign take off. People engage. You sell more product. There is an increased awareness of your brand. After several weeks it will be over. The fever dies. The hashtags are used less. The video, even if it went viral, has significantly fewer clicks and shares. The long tail in this case is when people are still talking about your brand, your product, and your campaign for longer, even if the numbers are lower.

When you engage influencers, particularly those with invested affinity for your brand, the conversation continues without your involvement. The traditional view of a marketing strategy would end once the campaign is over. With influencer marketing, it goes longer. How do you turn these new consumers into brand advocates? How do you engage them to leverage their voices and their social media presence to help your brand? It's through authentic engagement and investment in building relationships. When you create the long-term relationships I recommend, the long tail continues to work for your brand after your campaign has concluded. This is especially true in certain content media, where influencer blog content, Pinterest pins, and even hashtagged images can have a very long lifespan in the search engines of each network due to the digital authority an influencer might have.

In earlier chapters, I detailed how the control over the buyer's journey has changed. Throwing more money at traditional marketing channels doesn't have the same impact it used to because of the democratization of media consumption. Just as there are no longer three major television networks controlling the flow of information, there are also various sources of information about your product outside your control. The journey doesn't end at purchase. Now the engagement continues. When someone goes to a store for a coffee, purchasing a coffee doesn't end the transaction: It continues on social media when they share the picture of the coffee on Instagram, promoting the coffee chain further. This is one of the reasons why companies are investing so much in customer experience marketing and customer success.

Taking advantage of the long tail provides benefits beyond just engagement and awareness. The time and money you've spent on a campaign, on videos or content, can now provide returns for longer without the same level of investment.

7

THE EMPLOYEE
AS INFLUENCER

While we are beginning to see the emergence of what we call employee advocacy programs at larger enterprises, the concept of utilizing employees as influencers is still a largely untapped resource. One reason might be the complex legal issues that it entails, and needless to say I urge you to consult with your legal team should you wish to engage with employees in the method I suggest in this chapter. However, when looking at engaging with influencers or exploring ways of expanding their brand's social media community, most people overlook the power of their employee base and the strength already in their company. Employees already have an affinity for your brand. They care about your message, and—as shown in some cases I'll discuss later in the chapter—they're actually the group that is best able to deliver your message.

There are some deeper implications of employee advocacy programs to consider from an HR standpoint. It's not uncommon for companies to have a blanket ban on employees mentioning or discussing the brand online. Many large brands involve nondisclosure agreements from the beginning of employment. These agreements certainly make sense and there are many understandable reasons for them, but engaging employees on social media in the right spirit can bring many benefits. Issues regarding keeping the program optional and allowing employees to keep their social media private should also be considered. It won't suit every kind of company just as it won't suit every employee. All of these points must be firmly understood by both the company and the employee before engaging in an advocacy program. That's why it's a good idea to run the concept through HR. The programs considered here are good examples of setting up the opportunity for employee advocacy and seeing how different approaches benefited different companies.

Starting your influencer relationships with those close to the brand, such as employees and existing fans, smooths the slide into engaging influencers. It also presents opportunities to experiment and develop before going outside. It can serve as a test run or a way to gauge the success of certain approaches. Engaging those already with a vested interest gives you an idea of how influencer relationships work for your brand. Finding this way to communicate with your community is essential to making the relationship with your influencers work. How one brand or company approaches influencers won't necessarily translate to another brand, even within the same sector. Learning this and experimenting with these strategies using people close in your affinity circle is a great test to see what can be replicated outside. And it can certainly bring results that might surprise you.

THE SURPRISING REACH OF EMPLOYEES

One of my favorite perspectives on this potential of employees as influencers is perfectly captured in this quote from Nathan Egan, the CEO and Founder of the now defunct PeopleLinx:

> Your organization has thousands of websites, not just one. . . .
> Your employees are the long tail of your brand identity.[1]

This is the crux of why employees are such a powerful but often untapped source of organic and influential engagement. Each of your employees has a social media following. It's entirely possible that several of your employees are already influencers. They may have entire communities following them that you're unaware of, and when you tap into this it's a win–win situation. When you engage an employee as an influencer, they can speak authoritatively on your message in an authentic way to their already engaged audience.

Furthermore, employees hold a unique position for your brand from a message and engagement perspective. Employees are more trusted than corporate voices. Studies have shown that employees are more trusted than the CEO, the marketing and advertising departments, and more than an industry analyst.[2]

Research published by Ken Irons has shown that as much as 70 percent of brand perception is determined by interactions with people.[3] When someone steps inside a showroom, the perception that they most strongly take away is the interaction with people. This isn't even taking into account interactions that led them to approach the showroom in the first place. This truth about brand perception used to be true mostly for customer-facing employees. It was drilled into salespeople or brand representatives who interacted with other businesses and customers to close the sale. Now it's not just the customer-facing employees. And more recently, it's not just interactions in person. It's interactions online. Every employee who is connected with your brand online is now a chance to strengthen your brand identity.

Now that we live in a digital world, the chance of interaction with your brand outside of the usual place of purchasing and traditional contact has increased. It's not a liability: This is opportunity. Whenever an employee says they work at your brand on their social media they are a representative; we form a brand perception based on what that person says or does on social media. It's inevitable. This works differently on different platforms, of course. People don't always list their employer or company on Facebook or Twitter. On LinkedIn, it's essential.

This gives your brand online voices and multiple points of contact, empowering you to be represented and to promote your message with far more coverage than before. A Pew survey into the demographics of social media found, like most surveys into this figure, that social media's most active demographic is under age thirty.[4] The engagement isn't surprising. Older users, in their thirties and forties, who began using social media when it first took root in our lives (even before Facebook was around and Myspace was the big thing) are now in the second large cohort engaged in social media. The percentage of engagement is a little lower than those in their early twenties, but still well over three-quarters. The study also showed that the fifty-to-sixty-four-year-old group engaged in social media at a rate over 50 percent. Social media is mainstream. Since all of your employees are probably using it, and some of them might be using it better than your brand can, it pays to engage your employees.

THE FOUR KINDS OF DIGITAL MEDIA

When looking to promote or spread a message there are four kinds of digital media you can engage with. These four often have different approaches and ways of working. There are some points where they converge, but they can still be described separately. As with the levels of affinity, it's wise to engage across a variety of these. What I will be referring to is actually the traditional division of digital media into paid, owned, and earned media.

Paid media is that which you engage with through paid measures, such as online advertising and paid social. The media is run or owned by outside parties who make money through this paid message amplification.

Owned media is the media that you own. Your website or app is in this category. There are also your own social media sites, Twitter and Facebook feeds, and any newsletters or publications you own.

Earned media encompasses those forums or media where you have earned coverage—the kind where others talk about you, your brand, or your product in other newsletters or publications and increasingly through shared social media posts or blogs.

The concept of **Employed Media** emerged several years ago (see Figure 7.1).[5] Coverage or message amplification coming from your employees, and sometimes their own content creation, presents a huge opportunity. Similar to earned media, there is an element of earning, and like paid there is often some incentive attached (although not paid per se), but employed media is in its own category. It's organic, it's trusted, and the bigger the company the more impactful it can be.

If your employees are predominantly from a generation other than your executives, there's a strong chance your employees have a better grasp of newer social media platforms such as Twitch, Snapchat, or Instagram. Engaging these employees to

THE EMERGENCE OF EMPLOYED MEDIA

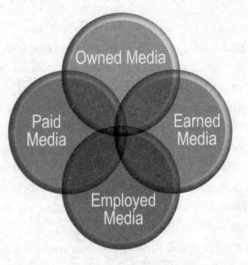

SOURCE: DOUG KESSLER / CONTENT MARKETING INSTITUTE

Figure 7.1

share your message in this environment exposes a new audience and demographic to your message that would otherwise be unreachable in your current social media strategy.

Employee advocacy taps into the communities your employees have created. This presents the opportunity to expose your message to a new audience organically, authentically, and from a trusted voice. The average overlap of your employee followers and company followers is rarely even as high as 10 percent. A study showed that the crossover for Cisco, whose employees had ten times more followers than their corporate accounts at the time, sat at only 2 percent.[6]

Prudential Financial saw this potential when they engaged in an employee advocacy program aimed at their employees' LinkedIn pages.[7] The company recognized that they had 15,000 employees on the LinkedIn platform. There was an average of

160 connections per employee, meaning the possible spread of a message—not considering overlap of these connections—could be as high as 2.4 million for each message. Your employees' network is larger than you think. Even for a small business with only ten employees, taking that same number of 160 connections per employee puts the potential audience at another 1,600 people that you might not otherwise engage.

It's also worth noting that these numbers are conservative estimates. A Finnish study showed that on average, employees have 420 Facebook friends, 400 LinkedIn connections and 360 Twitter followers.[8] For that same company with ten employees, reaching out over these three platforms and ignoring any overlap, that message has reached a potential audience of almost 12,000. One study by IBM showed that content shared by employees generated leads that converted at a rate of seven times more than those that came from content shared from their company account.[9] Employee advocacy helps build your brand.

LEVERAGING THE POWER OF EMPLOYEE VOICES

Leveraging your employees' voices can be an extension of your existing employee advocacy program—and if you don't have one yet then you should definitely be looking into developing one. When the groundwork has been laid and the foundation of employee advocacy has been set, then engaging with your employees as influencers can begin.

At the heart of all employee advocacy programs is the notion that employees can be leveraged as brand ambassadors on social media and engaged in spreading content from your brand. Popular news stories like charity events, industry and product innovation, awards, and other industry success can be amplified by being shared by employees. The key is adding incentive to engage with your employees.

Like all influencer campaigns, employee advocacy starts by opening the communication for an authentic interaction. What can you offer the employee? What can you bring to the table that incentivizes them to open their private networks to you? It's also imperative to keep in mind that truly utilizing your employees as influencers is more than just establishing an advocacy program and certainly more than asking your employees to share your ads or promotions to their friends and family. How could you best collaborate with them? They should want to share the content if they're proud of the news around the brand or if they think it's cool. They won't automatically want to give the brand greater visibility in their own communities.

The Iceland supermarket in the United Kingdom utilized their mobile app, the Insider Iceland app, to give employees access to news articles and information that they were encouraged to share on Twitter and Facebook.[10] If an employee desired, there was information that could be shared each day. Over three months, Iceland supermarkets were able to develop 450 employee advocates who shared their news and generated 37 million social media impressions. The chain's mobile app made it easy for employees to share the information that the chain made available to them while allowing the chain to measure accurate KPI information. Engaging employees in this way involved creating content for them to share that covered the desired information but didn't feel like an advertisement. Employees don't want to share your ads, and merely sharing ads won't give you much engagement.

CATHAY PACIFIC

THE KNOWLEDGE THAT EMPLOYEES HAVE ABOUT your products, as well as having existing brand affinity, places employees in a unique place as influencers. It's likely that your employees are already serving as advocates when friends who know which industry they work in ask for advice. Word of mouth has always been an important way of making a buying decision. How can you leverage employee voices to reinforce your brand message? What can you give to employees to make them brand advocates?

Cathay Pacific began their employee advocacy program when they realized that their employees, by the nature of their jobs, were extremely well-traveled.[11] This aligned with the brand values and the emphasis of an upcoming campaign. Employees have amazing stories to tell. Engaging with their audiences presents another way to reach those audiences on social media. As a strong source of information, and an extension of the time-tested concept of word of mouth, employees were approached to help share information about the company. The program was mentioned through the company's communications, which led to a lot of employees engaging with the advocacy program. To the surprise of many, the most avid supporters and most frequent posters were not flight attendants or pilots, but an engineer in Hong Kong and a staffer in the call center in Mumbai.

To incentivize the advocacy program, the airline gives points to those who share news and articles; the points can be redeemed for products, similar to air miles. Once each quarter the company also runs a competition giving away tickets for sponsored events, such as world sporting championships. (The nature of being a global company presents problems in that what is interesting to someone in Hong Kong might not be an incentive to those in San Francisco.) Cathay Pacific also keeps the information feed about the industry, focusing three-quarters of the posts on travel rather than company-specific news. Much of the content comes from outside the company, minimizing the need to constantly create content. The aim is to make it information that employees want to share with their friends and family on their personal social media pages.

Tools have been developed to help track the success of advocacy. The dashboard view of information that these tools provide shows the type of posts being shared and by whom. This information allows the company to refine the information and articles available to share. By working through the data and refining the approach, the brand ensures that only the most relevant and interesting articles and information become content, engaging employees more as they become brand advocates.

STARTING WITH THE FOUNDATION

Although employee advocacy programs begin with a marketing objective and with distinct sales-oriented goals, most companies have found success when combining their program with a strategy for increasing employee engagement. Other potential objectives include social selling, content marketing or amplification, brand awareness, reputation management, and social recruiting. These are all possible aims and goals of an employee advocacy program, but you can't do all of them: In order to most effectively leverage your employees' voices, you must decide what are the key goals for your brand and your program.

The next step—and the third section of this book will cover creating influencer programs in more detail—is preparing the infrastructure. There are things to consider and put in place that cover social media policy, information about not divulging content, nondisclosure agreements, and other guidelines. Much of this is common sense, like company trade secrets or negative comments, but it's wise to cover it. The programs that have shown the best results have largely come from companies that engaged training programs covering best practices and even taught their employees how to better leverage social media for their own professional branding and work. In fact, companies teaching their employees how to become more influential in social media might be a topic that would encourage many active social media user employees to join their program.

The heart of any social media engagement or employee as influencer programs is no different: It comes down to both the creation and sharing of content. This content can present difficulties to brands. Employees don't want to share the fact that you have a sale going on until Friday, or a two-for-one deal until the end of the month. The content has to be something that they want to share with their networks. They don't want to share ads. It's a give-and-take relationship, so you have to find what you can offer them, often in the terms of content. In some cases, content might even come from your employees. A plant nursery that I worked with in the past had a different employee every day of the week managing their social media profiles and posting content from their knowledge of flowers and shrubs.

There are a number of tools that make it easier for your employees to share the content you curate or create. What is important is making this content easy to share. The good news is that since employee as influencer programs are becoming more common, platforms are building their own apps to aid the transition. LinkedIn has its own platform called Elevate. Leading social media dashboard tools like Hootsuite (Amplify) and SproutSocial (Bambu) have also developed platforms for their customers to utilize for this specific objective. This not only helps make sharing it easy, it helps you schedule when certain news or content will be available.

To properly engage your employees, you need to offer an incentive for them to share your information with their communities. Although employees have an existing affinity for your brand, tapping into the employee as influencer is a different kind of relationship than an employer-to-employee relationship. It requires establishing a dialogue and listening to what your employees want in terms of partnering with you—and what you can offer. It has to become a collaborative and mutually beneficial initiative in order for it to be successful. This collaboration will also give you a chance to experiment and see what works best for your brand in terms of incentives and offers to engage and collaborate with the next levels of influencers.

8

THE SIXTEEN DIFFERENT WAYS TO COLLABORATE WITH INFLUENCERS

Engaging in relationships and leveraging other people to talk about your company and brand is the fundamental goal of all marketing. Influencer marketing presents new avenues to spread your message. At this point, most brands and businesses are engaged in social media marketing in some way. This means that you're already involved with elements of influencer marketing, whether you are aware of it or not. However, not actively engaging with influencers means the full potential of social media strategy goes unharnessed. Tapping into content curation, sharing other people's images or tweets is one method of engaging with influencers. Affiliate marketing is another example of influencer marketing.

In doing research for this book, I identified sixteen different ways in which any brand can collaborate with influencers. While they range in scope and goals, all are based on establishing a connection with people who yield some type of online influence you want to tap. Some of these strategies work well as a tentpole for a program and can be supported by other types on the list.

TRADITIONAL TYPES OF INFLUENCER MARKETING

Some of your traditional marketing activities might already include elements of influencer marketing without your realizing it.

A common and easy way of collaborating with influencers is **Gifting Swag**, or in football terms, the **Hail Mary**—mailing swag such as branded pens, coffee cups, t-shirts, USB drives, or key rings to an influencer and hoping they appreciated the gesture enough to mention your company in their social media posts. The obvious thinking is that when the influencer needs a USB or something to write down their next viral blog idea, your logo will be right in front of them. I call this a Hail Mary because it's similar to the last-second play in football, throwing the ball from the other end of the field and hoping it goes where you intend despite the extremely low odds. The pen or key ring is often something not needed by the influencer, unrelated to your own product, and often accompanied by a semi-personalized letter that sounds too generic and asks the influencer to post a hashtag that might be irrelevant to their personal brand.

Gifting Product is about sending your own product, not mere swag, in hopes the influencer will mention it in social media. I have experienced many gifting campaigns that aren't personal enough and don't consider the influencer specifically. It's throwing gifts into the wind. In this scenario, the product gifted is irrelevant. However, if you were to reach out to relevant influencers and actually ask if they would like the gift, requesting them to post about it to their community only if they found it recommendable, the success rate of such a program increases exponentially, especially when asking targeted influencers with the followers in your pinpointed demographic. When this is done right, the photos of real people using the product can make a powerful connection to the people you want to attract. The reviews and hashtags can be searched forever. Smart companies have stopped Hail Mary gifting and are finding new ways of working with relevant influencers, especially micro- and nano-influencers, who are often happy to post on social media in exchange for free product.

KLEANPLATE

ENGAGING INFLUENCERS TO GENERATE GROUND-level organic discussion through gifting product can be a highly effective strategy when properly planned and implemented.

Kleanplate is a niche health-food product making waffle and pancake mix high in protein. The mix is geared to body builders and fitness fanatics. The brand spent a lot of time and energy identifying influencers Kleanplate might appeal to, then reached out to those who they thought the brand would resonate the most for. The founder of the product wrote a personalized note to connect with each influencer, introducing the product. An impressive 86 percent of influencers who they contacted replied to their brief.

The brand reached out in an authentic manner, asking the influencers if they'd like to try the product and, if they liked it, to review it. The vetting had been done early on, and so the response rate was again impressive, a high 76 percent. Over four months, Kleanplate measured a 204 percent increase in website traffic, resulting in 14 times their previous sales volume.[1]

A **Giveaway or Sweepstakes** is another popular and tested method of influencer collaboration. This can be a combination of giving away and gifting for review, allowing the influencer to decide how they want to work with you and your product. Many influencers love doing giveaways if the product is relevant to their audience. It's a great way for them to add value to their community, give them some additional status, encourage additional engagement through the giveaway content, and can also help them build a larger email list. For you, it's a great way of increasing brand awareness and establishing a relationship with influencers.

LORD & TAYLOR

WITH SO MANY VOICES ON INSTAGRAM AND other networks, how do you make sure your posts stand out? Can repetition help you or hinder you? In order to promote their Design Lab collection, Lord & Taylor enlisted the help of a lot of Instagram fashionistas, opting for strength in numbers.[2]

They contacted fifty fashion Instagrammers and bloggers to post pictures wearing the same colorful paisley dress on the same weekend. The dress immediately sold out from Lord & Taylor.

The alternative aim, of promoting the Design Lab collection, also proved a success. Many of the posts collected more than a thousand likes, and some reached almost 15,000. The posts were paid, with some Instagrammers reportedly paid up to $4,000 for the single post. It's a fine example of a program where the ROI was measured in both sales and social media measurements.

One oversight Lord & Taylor made was not ensuring all influencers listed and marked the posts as paid content. Later edits to some posts made it clearer. There was some level of backlash where people posted comments on some influencers' streams questioning whether it was an ad or a paid post. The Federal Trade Commisson (FTC) investigated whether the brand had overstepped the line, and the issue was later settled, with Lord & Taylor, and every other company going forward, clearly stating in influencers' posts that they have been compensated.[3] In influencer marketing circles, this case study represents the first time the FTC cracked down on an influencer marketing campaign. Since then, brands have needed to ensure that all influencers who are paid with money or by receiving product clearly state in their Instagram and social media posts that their content is #sponsored or an #ad. This is a universal trend: The UK ad watchdog cautioned between two hundred and three hundred influencers for breaking similar rules.[4] This is an area where brands need to stay vigilant and make sure that the influencers they collaborate with are equally compliant.

If your product or service isn't easily given away, consider **Affiliate Marketing.** This is another example of leaving the communication open to find a middle ground. Maybe that product is too expensive to give away, but you can recruit your influencer as an affiliate marketer so they can still profit from it. Another advantage to affiliate marketing is the ability to track the influence of each participant through the unique tracking numbers you give them, allowing you to adjust future partnerships. The addition of Amazon Influencer Shops makes affiliate influencers an attractive option if you are trying to increase sales through Amazon.

Another angle is **Promotion Codes and Discounts**. This is where you talk to the influencer and, similarly to the affiliate marketing strategy, show them how sharing your information will help their community. You provide special discount codes just for their followers such as SCHAFFER25, which in this case might indicate a 25 percent discount to my followers. A discount code can provide value to communities you want to influence, and an often positive side effect of publishing discount codes is the plethora of couponing websites that will find and amplify your code across the internet. Naturally, providing discount codes to influencers can be mixed with other elements like affiliate marketing and with a giveaway to connect to influencers and their networks on multiple levels. The ability to measure and compare the performance of influencers through their publishing of these codes can help increase the effectiveness of your influencer marketing program over time.

CONTENT CREATION-CENTRIC TYPES OF INFLUENCER MARKETING

Content creation is an essential part of influencer marketing and building longer term relationships. As with the other strategies, it can be complementary to other approaches and can build on the ground each of them covers. Content strategies open up avenues to always having content on hand. You've always got something for your social media posts while establishing avenues for content distribution. Content creation does have aspects that favor B2B communication more than others. The content supports the buyer's journey, explaining why a lot of B2B companies engage with influencers in these ways. That being said, the visual challenges that social media marketing brings to brands have brought about a renaissance in consumer-facing brands leveraging user-generated content from influencers for visual social networks.

Developing a social media presence is an essential tool but maintaining a constant stream of content when you may not have enough of your own can be a major challenge to many companies. **Content Curation** is the answer to this. If you're going to curate the content of others to share on social media, why not curate the content of influencers as a way to begin a relationship with them? Not only does this solve the problem of always having great content to share with your followers, but it does the work of opening relationships and dialogue if you map it back to the influencers with whom you want to align yourself. It kills me when businesses reach out to me and want to work with me, and maybe I've shared their content in the past, but they haven't shared mine or interacted with me in any way. Laying the groundwork early can pay off later when you need to call on that fledgling relationship. Curating the content of influencers is the easiest way, and often a preferred way, to start a relationship.

Content curation can be a powerful social signal to send influencers. I still haven't forgotten the day that Emirates Airline reshared my Instagram Story of my arrival on an Emirates flight in Dubai to their fans. Social media users do not expect brands to directly engage with them, so when this happens, it has the potential to be an unforgettable and continual top-of-mind activity that can separate your company from the others that have yet to utilize this tactic.

Should there be certain influencer content that you curate or repost that garners great engagement from your community, you might want to consider a relationship where you hire the influencer to actually create content for you as part of your **Content Creation Outsourcing**. More and more brands are leveraging influencers in this way, not as a collaborator in the amplification of content, but utilizing their skills for the actual creation of the content itself. Influencers are often excellent content creators, so collaborating with them in this fashion should not be overlooked. As content creation often carries with it a budget, this might be an easy way to begin a paid engagement with an influencer.

Just as you are amplifying the content of influencers when you curate their content, having influencers repost or share your content with their community is **Content Amplification**. If you've done the work of content curation already, then having your own posts amplified through the relationships you've already made is a logical next step. Content amplification often carries a paid component. This can be a great strategy for when you don't have an organic relationship yet. It's also important to look at smaller influencers who might have a lesser reach but could be in a position to share your content with a growing community by agreeing to promote their content in the future. It can at least guarantee that some eyeballs from the influencer's community have a chance at engaging with your content.

Content amplification is often used in coordination with other types of influencer campaigns, often to support the content that the influencers publish. In other words, brands will reach out to their pool of influencers asking them to simply amplify the content that other influencers have created about their brand.

One of the most viral content elements we see is **Content Co-Creation**, often in the form of round-up posts where you collect your favorite ten or fifteen ideas on a topic.[5] These are popular but numerous at this point. It's not something I would suggest having as a main campaign, but some have found great results utilizing them, including a Norwegian blogger who gained 20,000+ page views in six days and ended up ranking #4 on Google for the competitive keyword phrase "productivity tip."[6]

Taking co-creation one step further brings us to **Content Sourcing.** Here you invite the influencer to contribute to your blog, Instagram feed, or do an interview. This doesn't necessarily have to have a paid component, but it certainly could include one. The validation from a third-party expert brings benefits including credibility and some help in amplification. When an influencer is featured on your site, they will link it to their network and community. Sourcing content in this way covers a lot of ground and gives a lot back to the influencer in return, establishing the relationship in both directions.

Finally, we come to **Sponsored Content Distribution,** often a paid element of content amplification. This is for when you've created content about your product or service and want it shared as is. We often see these with infographics that are nicely designed with some well laid-out information, but it could be done with blog posts, images, or videos as well. Contacting an influencer who you have already established a relationship with and asking them to publish your content on their profile can be one of the best ways to reach their communities. Having an influencer share content also brings an element of validation to your product. This strategy involves setting the foundation of the relationship beforehand. As I said before, reaching out to an influencer to share your content as the first communication with that person is more than likely going to end up with a no. This complements content curation particularly well and can be a payoff to the curation set up.

Sponsored Content Distribution is often executed together with Gifting Product, and when done in this way, influencers are often allowed to describe the product and service in their own voice based on their own experience rather than simply publishing the words and images of others. The trend towards employing micro- and nano-influencers has helped push companies into tapping into the authenticity of the influencer voice through this method of collaboration. As Sponsored Content Distribution will involve a monetary transaction, brands will place parameters on what they can or shouldn't mention in their social media post as well as hashtags to use and other necessary details that they might not be able to require from the influencer if only Gifting Product.

Since content is the currency of social media, many bloggers might actually accept your content submissions for free as a guest blogger submission if they are keen to publish more content with an increased frequency. While there might be limitations to the links you can use and editorial content guidelines, if the sole reason is to get *your* content on *their* blog, make sure you look for information on how to submit a guest post on any given influencer's website. An example of this is the "Write for This Blog" link on my own website: https://nealschaffer.com /guest-post-for-this-blog/.

NEWER AND EXPERIMENTAL CAMPAIGNS

The remaining campaign types are either newer or experimental and thus might not be appropriate for every company. Regardless of campaign type, they can still be effective because at their heart is the simple idea that people trust other people more than companies.

The **Shout Out** is a type of campaign originating from Instagram. Similar to Content Distribution, an Instagram user is publishing your content on their profile. However, instead of your content becoming an integral part in the user's newsfeed, your promotion is usually deleted after a few hours or a day. This is an approach that might not be well suited for large brands but could definitely work for smaller businesses wanting to try something different and new. The Shout Out is very much an internet marketing type of approach and an experimental tactic but there are companies that buy sponsored blog posts and sponsored tweets; this is basically a sponsored Instagram post, albeit only temporarily. It's a for-fee service but some might offer a shout out for free in exchange. Who would offer this service? We live in an uber society, a gig economy, where there's a lot of side hustle going on. Anyone with a large following can make some extra money by hosting Shout Outs. Sites like Shoutcart can handle the monetary transaction, allowing you to identify the influencer with the demographic and community you want to reach.[7]

Does it work? Anecdotal results show there can certainly be a large benefit from a sponsored shout out depending on your KPIs. It has proven particularly beneficial for certain clothing or health products. Shout outs can be a ninja tactic to increasing your own community. The key here, as with all influencer campaigns, is to identify the influencer in the best position to connect to your target community and measure the results to determine if this type of campaign is right for your brand or not.

Another newer and experimental type of influencer marketing campaign is the **Account Take Over**, which started with the emerging popularity of Snapchat. Sour Patch Kids handing over control of its Snapchat account was extremely successful. Instagram is another social media platform where we see the takeover. The account take over puts your social media account in the hands of an influencer for a length of time, sometimes as short as a day or as long as a week. This lets the influencer do what they do best and run your social media while putting a human face on the brand for a limited period of time. It taps into the community the influencer brings, and injects the influencer's own personality. The influencer brings authenticity to the medium where the brand would have otherwise really struggled to deliver it. This is a strategy that has been well explored on the B2C context but can be adapted to the B2B context too.

An increasingly popular strategy for B2B brands to directly engage with influencers is through **Event Coverage**. Inviting influencers to your event with the agreement that they will tweet and cover it on social media effectively covers several bases. It promotes the event to wider networks in an authentic and personal way. Giving influencers free rein to tweet, snap, and Instagram the goings-on also means the event is well documented for posterity. It's a powerful strategy.

We can go further and offer the influencers free tickets for some guests in addition to themselves, or discount codes to their network to get more attendees. Asking the influencers to blog about the event beforehand can increase excitement leading up to the event. Inviting influencers to speak or moderate at the event incentivizes their own need to publicize the event themselves. I've been invited to events like Adobe Summit, Marketo Marketing Nation, and Cisco Live as an influencer or social ambassador. This is something that's becoming very popular. Asking an influencer to speak takes it one step further.

VMWORLD

THE CHALLENGE FOR EVERY BRAND IS GETTING a message out further than the immediate audience. This becomes even more difficult when you're holding a conference. No matter where an event is held, there will be a large part of the audience unable to attend. How can a brand engage with influencers to find innovative ways to present content, even to those who can't attend?

When planning VMWorld2017 in Barcelona, software company VMware worked with the influencer marketing company Onalytica and invited seventy-five targeted core influencers to the event with the agreement that the influencers would blog, tweet, and cover the conference on social media.[8] Having influencers, including media and industry professionals, cover the event gives insight into the happenings at the conference for the rest of the industry. The organic documentation covers angles and information that the organizers would not have identified or reached through their own means.

Like many gatherings of this nature, there were many who weren't able to get to Barcelona for the conference. This is where the influencers took their involvement a step further. When they realized the interest in the conference online by those who couldn't attend, the influencers approached VMware and proposed that the influencers themselves hold a Twitter chat, or CrowdChat, to tap into the online audience.

The VMWorld organizers listened to the influencers and their insights into how VMWorld could best reach an extended audience. By giving the influencers more control over the way the event was represented online, the conference found an organic way to engage with a part of their audience who would have otherwise only been watching the events unfold online.

The influencer-hosted and -moderated CrowdChat brought together 2,500 online participants. This generated 469 posts by influencers, spokespeople, customers, partners, and employees, reaching 1.3 million users. This led to a 20 percent increase in brand awareness.

These impressive results were the result of two different steps.

The first was being aware of the large range of influencers and spending time to track and investigate the suitability of influencers even if the audience for a particular influencer was smaller than others. VMware identified 2,500 influencers and tracked their interactions online and the content of their posts to identify 75 core influencers. This didn't necessarily mean the ones with the largest followings, but instead the ones whose followers and content were most aligned with what VMWorld showcased. Engaging with smaller industry expert influencers instead of the mainstream social media influencers provided very high value and credible content.

Building authentic relationships with these targeted influencers opened the door for a partnership where the influencers wanted to help VMWorld in their own way. The CrowdChat gave a platform for the influencers to showcase their expertise while increasing awareness of VMWorld and VMware.

This took understanding and trust in the work the influencers did and the willingness to give up control over some aspects of the conference. By listening to the influencers and tapping into the expertise these industry insiders brought to the event, VMware was able to build upon the reach of the event and build their community in ways they hadn't anticipated.

Events are by no means limited to B2B brands. In fact, some companies are taking the extra step of actually creating events specifically geared towards influencers to develop relationships with them. The event becomes a vehicle for building rapport, focused on the influencers. General Electric organized an Instawalk through one of their jet engine factories for selected Instagram photographers.[9] It gave GE the chance to view the factory through the influencers' own personalities and perspectives while providing a more authentic approach and reaching a wider community than GE could otherwise have engaged. The power of events to foster relationships with influencers, though, is not limited to brands targeting consumers.

RESTAURANTS MAKING EVENTS

WORD OF MOUTH HAS LONG BEEN THE CORNERstone of the restaurant business, and the development of foodie bloggers and Instagrammers has moved this to the online realm.

A series of New York street food style restaurants found benefits from engaging with food influencers.[10] Everyone likes food, and everyone likes knowing what is happening and where. In big cities like New York, food blogging and Instagramming are powerful tools. In most restaurants these days you'll see people trying to get the right angle of their food, not minding if it's a little cold when they eat it as long as they got the right shot. For every style of dining experience in each city there are multiple food blogs and Instagram accounts. Los Angeles is the home to Kogi BBQ, the first food truck to go viral in the earlier days of social media. In New York, many gourmet street food restaurants offering pizza, hamburgers, and hotdogs have found great success with influencer engagement. One restaurant engaged just five influencers and generated 32,350 Instagram engagements.

It comes down to knowing what your influencer wants. In the case of many food bloggers, it's simply a meal, but it might also be an insight into different angles of the food you prepare or something unique that they can bring their audience. Another factor is knowing what you can present. Organizing a food influencer event and bringing several influencers together, curating a night to show the influencers how much you care about your food, and connecting with them on a personal level can bring benefits that far outweigh the cost of preparing a meal for them.

An increasingly popular way restaurants are beginning to do this is similar to the Instawalks or Instameet style events where you host your selected influencers in the restaurant for a particular evening. After working through the initial levels of engagement and identifying which influencers to work with, restaurants host an event specifically catered to the bloggers or Instagrammers. Organizing such an event goes beyond simply giving the influencer a free meal. Designing a menu card or something that can be photographed, documented, and shared on Instagram is an excellent start. Everything will be documented and being able to curate the content to better showcase the values of your brand and the style of your restaurant, while giving the influencers something to reinforce exclusivity, is essential. This might include unique cocktails or side dishes for the evening, again designed to be something that influencers will take photographs of and share. Having multiple meals made up—some to be photographed, and others to be tasted—could be another option.

From your end there may be certain requirements you have from the influencer. For instance, you might want to ask them to publish the content within a week or negotiate the rights to their images and content so you can publish it again at a later date. By engaging multiple influencers, particularly those who are strong voices in the demographic or the location you're aiming to reach, can help with the illusion that your restaurant is *everywhere*, and that *everyone* is talking about the new dishes you offer.

Pushing past a single event and really tapping into the idea of a long-term collaborative relationship with an influencer leads us to the **Brand Ambassador** strategy where the company/influencer relationship is undertaken with a much different focus. A brand ambassador strategy aims to develop a relationship with influencers who you can engage with on an as-needed basis throughout the year, pushing far beyond the single campaign approach and into deeper relationship territory. Opening up your brand in such a way involves trust in the influencer and the relationship. It involves investment on a personal level. The brand ambassador presents different possibilities of collaboration including the possibility of bringing the influencers into your team regularly as advisors. This way you can learn from them too, especially if they're thought leaders or sought-out experts or celebrities in the industry. After all, there's a reason you've chosen them as an influencer out of the others you shortlisted. Why not develop that relationship to be beneficial in both directions?

When All Nippon Airways wanted to spread the news about their being the first to fly the Boeing 787 as well as the new Inspiration of Japan service that they introduced on a few routes between North America and Japan, they contacted four influencers, including myself, and engaged with us in a deep way. We were given a tour and had the chance to interview engineers at their Tokyo Haneda Airport maintenance facility, attended cabin attendant school and served as passenger models, met with their brand consultant who was responsible for all the small details in the new inflight service, had a chance to fly in the new 787 which at the time was only flying on two domestic routes in Japan, and even had a team meeting with their marketing division about the latest social media trends. Naturally we shared all this with our communities. We were flown out again in collaboration with the Okinawa Tourist Board when All Nippon Airlines wanted to promote their Okinawa routes. Brand Ambassadorships are an awesome way to engage with influencers, and influencers are essentially the medium of social media marketing. This takes the influencer engagement one step further to convert the influencer into a true brand advocate.

The final type of influencer marketing is a trend that I can see will shape the future a lot more: a complete **Product Collaboration** between companies and influencers. Influencers are often in it for an end game that will achieve the monetization of their communities. Most influencers will work with companies and brands and get some money for sponsored posts and other strategies mentioned in this list. But at the end of the day they want to have their own product, just like any other business. As influencers look for ways to step into consumer products or to monetize their followers, Product Collaboration is an obvious step. It's a step or two beyond Brand Ambassadorship and involves actually working with the influencer to develop product, using their name and their input so they're part of the selling process, too. It allows brands who are open and innovative to work with influencers to develop new ideas and products to reach other communities that haven't been reached.

Those brands who work with influencers collaboratively are the way of the future. The influencers feel like it's their own product and share profits. This approach has taken a strong hold in Chinese online shopping, where five of the top female clothing brands were founded by influencers. When a brand can engage with influencers and develop a product with their name on it, specifically for their fan base, it will be the ultimate in personalization for influencers.

Much more recently this has begun to emerge in the United States. From Target's children's apparel line being designed by Gen Z influencers to BandAid leveraging lifestyle blogger and influencer Joy Cho to create bandages with playful colorful designs, brands realize that product collaboration is the ultimate way to develop a deep, mutually beneficial long-term relationship with sought-out influencers.[11] It results in better content, more authenticity, and at the end of the day, more engagement and trust for both influencer and brands.

Product collaborations aren't limited to younger or lifestyle influencers. Best-selling author and marketing influencer Gary Vaynerchuk collaborated with the iconic tennis shoe company K-Swiss on a shoe released at the end of 2017.[12] Vaynerchuk made his name as an author and influencer, staking out his position on social media over the last decade. His social media presence across various platforms caught the attention of K-Swiss when they recognized that he reached the same demographic K-Swiss was targeting—"the next generation of hustlers and go-getters." The partnership was perfect for both parties. Vaynerchuk designed two shoes for K-Swiss that were launched at the end of 2017, and another in the middle of 2018. The co-creation brings the creative power of both parties to the product, allowing the product and launch to harness the collective power of both influencer and brand in creation and in marketing. Beyond non-athlete celebrity shoe deals like Justin Bieber and Adidas, and Kanye West with both Adidas and Nike, this marks a strong move toward influencers being recognized as a viable collaborating partner because of the influence they have established. It's a trend that I am sure we will see a lot more of in the coming years.

In fact, Amazon's launch of their "The Drop" influencer project signals that influencer-influenced products might become more mainstream sooner than you might think.[13] Tapping into ecommerce trends and the popular trend of "pop-up shops," The Drop teams up with fashion influencers to create made-to-order products that are on sale for only thirty hours. All of these product collaboration examples, including Amazon's and Taobao's, come from the fashion world, but it won't be long before other industries catch on and begin to collaborate with influencers in a similar fashion.

PART THREE

HOW TO WORK WITH INFLUENCERS TO GENERATE MASSIVE RESULTS

At this point, the compelling potential value that influencer marketing brings is clear. The shift in the marketing environment has changed how brands and consumers interact, making scope and sheer scale of influencer marketing beneficial for nearly any business to tap into.

Whether you're working with traditional marketing, digital or social media marketing strategies, or influencer marketing methods, your goal is to increase your own influence within a specific target audience. Let's look now at the specifics of how businesses can leverage influencer marketing to spread their message to millions of people.

Many businesses simply reach out to influencers with no game plan or spend their budget on influencers after being convinced to do so by their agency. There's much more to influencer marketing than just outreach. The democratized social media space calls for different rules of engagement. Influencer marketing, in all its guises, is ultimately about human connection, relationships, and partnerships. It's about beginning a dialogue and finding how to work with an influencer beyond ad spend. When executed with care and development, influencer marketing can reach far beyond the scope of traditional marketing.

This section covers the information you need to be able to create, execute, and maximize the return of your influencer marketing program, showing you how to invest not just money in marketing but energy into relationships that will return more than you'd expect from ad spend. If done right, the efforts you put into your influencer marketing program should provide you benefits for years to come.

9

TO BUY
OR TO BUILD

The entire focus of marketing is anchored to the concept of return on investment, of a gain in market or sales in some way. Where influencer marketing differs, of course, is in the ability to engage organically to provide those returns. It also holds a certain unique status in that it's leveraging the voices of others that can provide long-term returns that are otherwise unattainable with a short-term advertising campaign.

There is a concept I addressed in my previous book, *Maximize Your Social*: Why pay for social media when it's free?[1] It's a valid question. The same point can be raised about influencer marketing. Connecting on social media costs nothing. So, the question remains: Why pay?

If we step back and look at influencer marketing as an extension of your social media strategy, then we can understand the context better. When social media first made an impact, some companies experienced social media engagement so intensely that they diverted their company site URLs to their Facebook pages. I would not suggest that companies replace their website with a redirection to a social media site.

There is a large amount you can do with social marketing organically, without paying a cent. Building and developing a community that is interested in your message is a fundamental social media strategy. However, there are times when that's not enough. There are times when you have a campaign you want to push further, or a demographic you want to connect with more than your community allows. Paid social allows you to boost what you do organically. Where social media is the amplifier to your message, paid social is the accelerator.

Paid social allows you to get where you want faster. Whatever you're promoting, whatever metric you use to measure success of engagement—whether it's a sale or building a community or generating clicks on a link, or more people going to the store—with paid social and a bit of money you will get to the result sooner. Paid social has become so important that some companies now separate their social media department into paid and organic, both with different aims, methods, and objectives, to garner the results they're looking for from both.

Paid social complements organic social. Organic social by itself will only get you so far. However, you can't only do paid social. There must be some organic presence and, ideally, engagement. If your profile doesn't replicate your message and your community doesn't reflect the message and idea shown in your promotions or ads, then you lose credibility. People will go to your profile. If your campaign pushes an image of a large company and they see that you only have 150 followers, then your brand identity and credibility take a hit. At that point the message, and the cost that you've invested to promote that message, is all for naught.

When you think of growing your brand and social media presence in terms of growing a crop, the analogy becomes clear.

It's more than just saying that you reap what you sow. When everything is growing steadily, and you're happy with the rainfall and the results it's bringing, then you don't need anything else. That's organic growth. But sometimes you need something to boost that. You need to add something extra from the fountain. You dip the bucket into the well, or turn on the faucet a little, and let some more water into the crop to help it grow. Paid social is dipping into the well. It's allowing some more water to flow into the crop to help you get to the next step more quickly than waiting for the rain.

BUILDING PAID SOCIAL

Paid social has become more important in recent years simply because, as mentioned before, the algorithms on social media networks work against businesses. Social media is for people, not businesses. So the reality of the landscape is that social media is pay to play. In terms of older days, consider when being in front of customers meant that companies simply needed to be listed in the phone book. It was free to be listed but making your brand stand out cost a bit more money for a bigger ad or larger type. Paid social is how you can stand out.

There are definitely some networks with much more of an organic engagement level but when looking beyond the immediate present and projecting even for the short-term future, we see that things will change. Brands need to adjust how they communicate their message. Only a few years ago it was easier to spread your message on social media. Now there is much more distrust in advertisements. There are entire demographics turning away from the usual methods brands use to communicate.

The problem with paid social is that when ads become prominent, invading the space of social media users, then the eyeballs you target turn off. Social media platforms change their algorithms to change the way users interact with ads. When scrolling through feeds it's easy to spot an ad. There is a format to them. They stand out. They might be rare to start with, or novel in their design, but they quickly become more prevalent and water down the effectiveness.

Influencer marketing engagement supports both organic social and paid social. It's the third prong of the social media strategy. A survey by Relatable showed that 94 percent of marketers found influencer marketing to be an effective form of marketing.[2] Furthermore, eight out of ten brands will have a dedicated budget for influencer marketing in the next year. Influencer marketing is quickly evolving from a subset of a campaign budget for having its own integral line item in the marketing budget of a growing number of brands.

AGENCIES OR GOING IT ALONE

Now that you're committed to influencer marketing, you need to take a look in-house and decide if you are going to invest internal resources or hire an agency to develop relationships with influencers.

Agencies are often looked to as the middlemen when dealing with influencers. This can be a useful approach, but is largely a replication of the traditional celebrity endorsement model. Engaging with influencers is fundamentally different and you may find a varied approach works better. It's a long-term commitment with a long-term view on benefits. There are platforms that make working with influencers easy (which will be covered in depth later). Agencies can be a helpful intermediary between a brand and an influencer where there is confusion and can be leveraged for their experience. For those companies new to influencer marketing, who lack the internal resources to properly follow the guidance in this book, or who simply haven't seen good results from their influencer program, working with an agency with a strong track record of influencer collaborations is the quickest way to effectively work with influencers while driving business results.

Agencies can play an important role in your influencer marketing program only if they have a deep understanding of your brand culture, target market, and specific requirements your brand might have for influencer engagement. The current data suggest that nearly a quarter of businesses are still engaging with influencers through agencies.[3]

A client of mine who was a business author worked with an agency to manage his social media marketing. The agency began pushing influencer marketing. This could open up a new range of ways the author could share his message. However, the influencers the agency suggested, and with whom they already had relationships, were action sports athletes and millennial celebrities who didn't fit with the business author's demographic. These influencers definitely had a grasp of social media and their audience, but they did not have the audience the business author shared or wanted to reach. For this reason, they were irrelevant from the very start. It would be analogous to advertising for a business book on a billboard at a skate park. The billboard would be ideal for some shoe brands or lifestyle brands, but not for a business author.

This is an example of an agency pushing talent as influencers, or the other way around. While there is a lot of money to be made in influencer marketing, missteps like this can cost more than they will benefit.

Another often held misconception is that you have to pay a lot of money when working with influencers. Stories about leading Instagram influencers and the figures they pull in for each post further this myth. There are certainly people making a substantial amount of money, and brands paying it, but you're not required to pay in order to work with influencers. Agencies, brands, and influencers might work together for a short-term one-night stand but this is a trend that is changing. Brands and influencers alike recognize the value of building and developing long-term relationships. A study published by Activate showed that nearly 50 percent of marketers are working with influencers for six months or longer.[3] The more investment you put into organically building relationships and hopefully turning influencers into advocates, the more benefits you will reap later. You will already have the relationships to draw on when you need to return to the fountain.

Buying influence is traditionally more of a B2C approach stemming from the celebrity endorsement model. The audience can identify an ad and recognize its transactional nature. The bought influence is often one-time or short-term. Building is often linked more to the B2B brands and products, stemming from working with ecosystem and distributor partners. In recent years we have been seeing a convergence where both sectors are realizing the benefits of blending both for their influencer program.

By engaging with influencers in an organic way, approaching them as people, and building relationships, the returns have the potential to be long-term. You convert influencers to advocates, going beyond the campaign you have in front of you. The influencer becomes a partner. This is a win/win situation and yields the highest return on investment. When it's a one-time transaction, everything you've taught someone about your brand, all the work you've done to find affinity and alignment, is gone with one swing of the bat. Working longer with an influencer brings other benefits, such as learning and tapping into what they know about their community—and in some cases their expertise in fields you want to reach—along with the community's needs from your brand and product. The investment here is mostly time. One report showed that at one time 69 percent of companies hadn't paid influencers.[4] Today influencers are more numerous and the industry mainstream, so your experience might differ. This figure does hint at the potentially many benefits to be had outside of a monetary transaction, including the increasingly popular product gifting to micro- and nano-influencers.

Marketing plans for companies engaging with influencers outline different line items. They list organic social and paid social. For influencer marketing, it's not about a campaign. Instead, it's about building a pool of influencers you can work with and return to when you need. It's a two-sided coin giving you options. Investing money for the initial transaction, using some ad spend for paid influencer marketing with a view toward establishing long-term relationships, allows you toward connect with influencers and keep water in the well for when you need it. Each influencer wants something different, and the approach will vary. But approaching them individually, as time-consuming as it can be, leads to a return that can surprise you.

CORA

ENLISTING THE HELP OF INFLUENCERS DOESN'T always have to cost money. What can you give to an influencer that's not monetary? Why would they work with you while being unpaid?

Smaller influencers, those with fewer than 10,000 followers, often come with a more dedicated following than those with a large following. The engagement is stronger, and at a lower cost. There are ways you can leverage their voice for no monetary transaction, by engaging them with some- thing they can give their community.

Cora sells a monthly subscription to organic tampons. The brand decided to enlist the services of micro-influencers. Cora sent each chosen micro-influencer their product and requested that they include the product in their posts.[5] Taking engaging pictures of tampons might be a challenge, but when an influencer is visually literate and able to work it in with their lifestyle pictures, the content is seamless.

The posts engaged with the influencer's followers, spark- ing conversation and more referrals to the brand's subscrip- tion services. The posts for Cora were unpaid: The only price for the brand was gifting and shipping product.

THE FACTORS AFFECTING INFLUENCER SPEND

Despite all the discussion about influencer marketing requiring a different approach, and having a different mind-set when looking at costs, the answer still comes down to figures. In or- der to have a guide, I'll present two approaches that I've found marketers take when considering the cost of influencer market- ing programs.

To pay for your influencer marketing program you will have to take money from somewhere. Fitting it into your al- ready existing social media marketing budget or your broader marketing budget only requires a reallocation of funds. It doesn't need a new budget to be created from scratch. This is another example of how influencer marketing complements everything but replaces nothing. Until there is a visible ROI on this spend, brands naturally have their doubts about in- creasing the budget. For more aggressive companies, or perhaps for younger startups who have seen the ROI early on, it's not uncommon to spend over 20 percent of the marketing budget on influencer programs.

According to an Influencer Marketing Hub report, only 19 percent of marketers interviewed spent 10 percent or less of their marketing budget on influencers.[6] The survey showed that a majority of marketers were spending over 20 percent of the marketing budget on influencers. In fact, 11 percent of marketers were already allocating more than 40 percent of their marketing budget to influencer marketing. Use these figures as a guide. It's a barometer to measure and show how your spend and marketing budget line up with others doing the same work.

A separate study by Mediakix that looked at the specific figure spent instead of spending as a percentage indicated that about half of budgets for influencer marketing fall under $50,000.[7] In fact, 34 percent of influencer marketing budgets fell under $10,000. These figures, however, don't necessarily take into account the gifted product given nor personnel and agency expense to manage influencer relationships.

With the spend as a part of the budget, there are other factors to consider when negotiating influencer rates (see Figure 9.1). Just as each influencer requires a level of individual connection, the way in which they are paid and what they are worth paying for your return varies with each case. There are certain points to consider for all of them.

The size and engagement of their audience is the first point that catches your attention. As mentioned earlier, a larger audience is not necessarily the best indicator. Influencers with a large following tend to have lower engagement. This is important to consider when negotiating the fee.

The level of products and experiences gifted also work into the transaction. If your brand is organizing a conference and

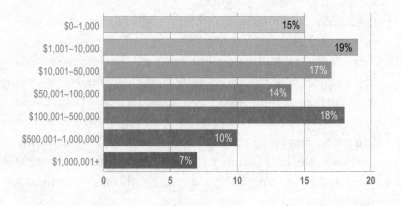

HOW MUCH IS YOUR INFLUENCER MARKETING BUDGET?

NOTE: DATA IS FOR 2019   SOURCE: MEDIAKIX

Figure 9.1

covering the accommodations and travel of the influencer, then there would be an expectation that the fee would be altered accordingly.

The usage rights to their material, which give you permission to use their images or videos in your own marketing content at a later date, also factors into the agreement. The content an influencer creates is legally their work, and it's entirely understandable that you would want to be able to use their content in your brand's social publishing.

The issue of exclusivity also comes into the conversation. If you require the influencer to not work with competitors or other brands in your market, and to take on your brand exclusively, then this is another element to consider. This might also work the other way, ensuring the influencer has exclusivity on content related to your brand to help them to continue building their relationships.

The length of partnership is the final element commonly listed. A longer term relationship lowers the initial fee with the understanding that the work will continue for monthly posts, or other conditions related to time commitment.

The factors taken into consideration when negotiating how much to pay can also be affected by the way in which you pay. There are other parts of the transaction that an influencer might be interested in and would suit your brand. The two most common—reported at 60 percent and 47 percent, respectively, by "a recent ACTIVATE State of Influencer Marketing" report—are a flat fee, and product in kind.[8] When asking an influencer to share your product on social media if they like it, it's common to give away samples or free memberships, and it's quite often a mixture of these. Post per engagement or click are a much less common way to pay but can be used as a way to measure results at the same time. The same can be said for affiliate marketing, essentially making the influencer your brand advocate. These models are also often presented in the negotiation as a mixture.

The standard rule of thumb that emerged as a guideline is that the cost of an influencer on Instagram is 1 percent of their followers.[9] For 10,000 followers, it costs $100 per post. For an influencer with 1,000 followers, the guide is $10 per post, and so on. This is a guide that has been around for a few years and is holding true even now, although of course it's subject to the factors mentioned above. Tools have emerged to guide marketers into how much to spend in engaging with influencers on Instagram from Influencer Marketing Hub and HypeAuditor.[10]

YouTube influencers tend to charge more, double that per follower. However many brands and agencies engaging with YouTube influencers prefer to measure by video views, and by this scale the price rate drops significantly. For influencers over certain levels of followers, the price can jump. This tends to happen when an influencer reaches over 100,000 followers,

and again at 1 million followers. I certainly stress the importance of researching the rate of engagement for influencers
with followers in this range. These figures are a guide, and for
some influencers who have a larger rate of engagement and
awareness among their followers, it's entirely plausible that
they charge a higher rate. On the other hand, you might be
able to negotiate with micro-influencers for an even lower rate.
It's going to be a case-by-case scenario, but just like understanding the going market rates in any economy, the more you
engage and build a track record, the better your understanding
will be for market rates.

The medium of the message is another key factor to consider.
What platform is the influencer on? Perhaps they're across several and can engage their followers in multiple ways. Blog posts
can range from under $50 to a few thousand dollars, depending
on factors considering content, followers, and readership. Twitter posts can have the same range. Some Instagram influencers
regularly receive several thousand dollars for a post. The type of
content or the message also affects the price, and this one boils
down to the usual marketing factors of demand. Travel, lifestyle, and fitness are big forums for influencers, and the big
topics that draw many followers.[11] Business bloggers or influencers who are heavily B2B have a much lower pool to publish
to, meaning their fee drops accordingly.

GOOD GREENS BARS

ALTHOUGH SOCIAL MEDIA AND THE INTERNET
allow brands to connect around the world, there is a definite
advantage in remaining local. How can you use local demographics to push the reach of your brand? What potential do
local influencers present?

Cleveland-based health food company Good Greens Bars looked locally first when promoting their protein bars.[12] Good Greens Bars mapped the Cleveland blogging landscape to see who the big voices were on the scene. They then approached the bloggers they identified and asked if they'd be interested in writing about their line of protein bars. Good Greens Bars looked to create longer term relationships from the very start and engaged the bloggers with that in mind.

Over thirty local bloggers worked with Good Greens Bars, guest blogging and otherwise promoting the product, in hopes of increasing the strength of Good Greens Bars' SEO and other online presence. The Alexa ranking increased to 1.7 million and the site increased to over 2,000 visitors a month, rising from a Google page rank of PR0 to PR3. Insights show that much of the traffic is local, coming from blog referrals. The four months following the campaign showed an increase in sales of 50 percent compared to the four months leading up to the campaign.

Engaging the local community in this hyper-local way helped Good Greens Bars hone in on a geographical demographic. This approach allowed the brand to spread their message in a strong and authentic way, highlighting their local origins, which delivered the return the brand was looking for beyond sales.

BEYOND THE TRANSACTION

When reaching out to influencers with whom you do not have a relationship, the transaction might be completely about a paid element. Establishing relationships can bring down the cost in monetary value because other things are being bartered in the deal. When we consider that we turn to paid social, and to influencer marketing by extension, when we need to augment other marketing, establishing relationships makes good business sense, on different levels.

For influencers, monetizing their following is certainly a major motivating factor, but the opportunity to connect with brands presents more possibilities than that. In fact, many new platforms for influencers have taken the monetary element out of the deal entirely and only offer product in kind as the incentive for working with brands. This concept of what, other than money, can you bring to the table is certainly something to consider when engaging with influencers. When looking to fill short-term goals, money might be the strongest incentive but when you have long-term goals then you and the influencer can create mutually beneficial relationships with an advocacy end-goal.

Identifying the right influencer(s) to work with is an art that will be covered in chapter 11. The essential thing you look for is an alignment between your brand values and beliefs and those of the influencer's content and community. This way you ensure you and the influencer want similar things. If the influencers you've chosen to work with get the most engagement when talking to their audience about your product, then you know you've chosen the right ones. This alignment, coupled with trust, leads to the best long-term return for your investment. Keeping these three points in mind—long-term goals, mutually beneficial relationship, and alignment of values and beliefs of brand with influencer content and audience—leads to a greater return over time. This is the same line of thinking as organic social. If you can achieve all your goals with organic social and don't have to rely on paid social, then that's an ideal situation. It means you've done organic extremely well. The same is true with influencer marketing. When an organic connection is made with the community, then the relationships blossom with less input from you.

Trust comes from building relationships, not from a one-time transaction. You strive to build trust as a brand with your customers, and this is done through multiple levels of engagement and multiple points of contact. This happens over time. The same is true with building relationships with influencers. The trust you want to build with your brand begins with the relationship you build with influencers. This is a point that I can't understate. Trust between you and the influencer leads to trust in the relationship, which snowballs into trust with the audience you're targeting.

The first step toward this is engaging with influencers as people first. Many marketers inadvertently make a fundamental mistake when they engage with influencers the first time by not treating them as people. They reach out to them with a business proposition as the first point of contact. This doesn't build trust. Instead, it shows that you're simply treating influencers as an advertising platform. Engaging with their content on a personal level is far more effective and opens the door to a relationship. As an influencer, I've had brands reach out to me offering clothing, stationery, or accessories as the first point of contact. The offers didn't engage with me and no further step was made to establish a relationship. The trust was not there to begin with.

You can't approach influencers as a platform like an advertising billboard or an ad spot. Someone who treats their audience as a platform is probably not going to be an effective vehicle to communicate your message. The engagement rate will be significantly lower than someone who holds more trust and has a better relationship with their audience. This, after all, is what you're looking for in an influencer and so it makes sense to take this into your own approach to connecting with the first point of contact. (This will be covered in much more depth in a later chapter.) What is important to understand here is that trust and relationships are both built over time. When you have established trust and a solid relationship with an influencer, there are added benefits over time. Perhaps they'll go above and beyond to promote your message because they have affinity for you. We enjoy working with people who trust us and understand our position. Influencers feel the same way.

So, the question of whether to buy or to build comes down to the fact that it's not one or the other. The truth is that depending on the scale of your program you might end up having to do both. The essential foundation of the entire enterprise is that the more you build the less you will need to buy over time—but buying opens doors and situations. Buying helps you build, allowing your crop to thrive while giving you something to draw upon when you go to the well, when you need to boost the organic growth.

Judging when to revisit the well, and how to measure your returns is another often misunderstood element of influencer marketing. It's understandable that everyone involved wants to comprehend the return on the budget. Understanding what's possible, and what counts as a return, is essential to knowing what progress you've made. That's why it's important to have a dedicated marketing strategy where you plot your own ROI before you even start.

EVEN THE SMALLEST OF BUSINESSES CAN LEVERAGE INFLUENCERS

THE POTENTIAL COSTS OF INFLUENCER MARKETING can sometimes scare away small businesses with limited budgets. Although engaging with influencers as a form of relationship development takes time, how can a small business engage with influencers for little or no money?

Revisiting the chapter on the different ways to collaborate with influencers, there are many paths for engaging with influencers for little or no spend:

1. **Gifting Product**—Optional combination with **Giveaway or Sweepstakes**. This will cost you the price of your product and potential shipping, but if you can find the right nano- or micro-influencer to post about it, this is a very cost-efficient form of influencer marketing.

2. **Affiliate Marketing**—Optional combination with **Promotion Codes and Discounts**. A completely cost-free way of working with influencers on a revenue-split basis. Not every influencer does affiliate marketing, but if you can offer a generous cut of your sales to the right influencer, you can see a direct impact on your sales.

3. **Content Curation**—The easiest way to begin a relationship through sending a powerful social signal while fulfilling the never-ending need to publish authentic content through your social channels at no cost.

4. **Content Co-Creation**—Asking an influencer for their opinion on a subject that you will later publish as a blog post or in a video is another free method of influencer collaboration.

5. **Sponsored Content Distribution**—While it will cost money to ask bloggers and social media users to publish your content on their website and feeds, working with the right targeted nano- and micro-influencers can bring this engagement below $100

per collaboration. Obviously, for those influential bloggers who accept guest posts, there is the potential that this could be free as well.

6. **Event Coverage**—If you're already doing an event, inviting targeted influencers who live locally, thus not requiring travel expense reimbursement, is an easy way to build influencer relationships in person that can lead to greater collaboration. There is also the option of creating an event with the objective of developing relationships with a selected group of influencers. New event creation and travel fees reimbursement for non-local influencers are the only potential costs your small business will have to incur.

DEVELOPING THE FOUNDATIONS OF AN INFLUENCER MARKETING STRATEGY

Before undertaking an influencer marketing-specific strategy, it's important to look at the grand scheme of your social media strategy to holistically understand the layout of the landscape and where influencers fit in. As with any business program, knowing the playing field is key to knowing how to strategize and engage. It's essential to look at this from a business perspective to understand what return you want from influencer engagement.

Social media is the new convergence of communication and information, the aftermath of which is the further democratization of communication and influence. Since influencers are dominant in social media, they hold the power to communicate and—obviously—influence on platforms. But there's a catch: The platforms are always evolving. Your strategy has to take into consideration this constantly changing environment rather than one goal.

Resisting the evolution of social media leaves your brand stuck in the past. By promoting a hashtag or campaign or product in the same way you engaged and promoted a photo last time, you miss the opportunity to engage and capitalize on the changing audience. The old Zen koan "You can't step in the same river twice" accepts the fluidity of the environment. The same applies here: "You can't run the same social media campaign twice." Engaging with influencers does, in some ways, help get around the pitfalls of a constantly changing footing.

EXPERIMENTING WITH EVOLUTION

In order to understand social media strategy and influencer plans, in general we have to understand and accept that the digital world is constantly evolving. Whatever you're doing in marketing can be complemented by the work you do on social media and with influencers. But since social media is a constantly changing and shifting beast, engaging effectively is more than just a challenge.

The majority of Facebook users are now over thirty-five.[1] The college students who it was first created for have grown up, while older age groups have taken up—some would say *hijacked*—the platform. It's no longer being used how it was first intended because the user demographic has shifted so drastically. The platform has evolved and added new features to engage with this shift and address changing user needs. The average demographic of Facebook is also affected by the rise of other platforms more appealing to younger users. Teenagers have other levels of engagement now.[2] They often have multiple Instagram accounts, one to tell their parents about and one for more personal use. They look in other places, especially Instagram, Snapchat, TikTok, and Tumblr. Many teenagers might never make a Facebook account.

Every culture uses social media in a different way, which also affects how platforms develop. In Japan, I've found that they use Facebook much like we use LinkedIn here in the United States. After going to a business meeting I've often received friend requests over Facebook that same night. It can be a little unsettling to see connection in an unfamiliar way on a forum normally used for different purposes, but it can also be a way to leverage Facebook for sales and not rely just on LinkedIn. This shows how social networks morph and merge into something that they weren't originally designed to be and don't remain static over time.

Twitter was the result of an internal hackathon at a podcasting company and the focus on someone's "status" or what people were doing at a given time, but it has evolved to become a network where news breaks.[3] The news of the aircraft landing on the Hudson River in New York broke on Twitter.[4] So did the news surrounding Whitney Houston's death.[5] Platforms will constantly evolve. Facebook was meant to be a communication tool among college students, not a forum that swayed public opinion in elections but, as evidenced by the need for CEO and founder Mark Zuckerberg's testimony in Congress and calls from the U.K. parliament, Facebook is much more than that now.[6] Social media platforms evolve due to pressures from both users and the functionality of the network. What people want changes and how people engage changes. Your effectiveness in engagement and the effectiveness of influencers always changes, too.

Social media is one grand experiment in audience engagement, and the same is true of influencers. To take a business perspective of this changing flow relies on engaging different levels of measurement and data points. The only way we can manage social media and influencer marketing is through looking at data. We have to understand that data and investment returns are always changing. So, we adapt. There is no tried-and-tested road, no stepping back in the same social media river. Paths that you would expect results from don't always work. Sometimes you'll find small audiences with huge levels of engagement, or the other way around. The only way to make it work is through experimenting and maintaining a data-driven approach. Luckily, we can measure how we experiment and develop our program, working with influencers and the changing landscape to engage our intended audience with our message.

TUNG BRUSH

CAN INFLUENCER MARKETING BE USEFUL TO HIT several goals at once? How can you leverage influencers in a personal way to test which products would be well-received in your market?

Tying an influencer campaign into an early stage of a new product launch can inspire more than just sales. TUNG Brush is the highest selling tongue brush in the United States.[7] When the brand was on the verge of adding a range of new colors to their catalogue, they tied the color-selection process into their influencer program in order to widen engagement. Increased presence on Instagram, sales, and color selection were all driving forces behind the campaign. This way of engagement brought results on many levels.

In order to increase their Instagram presence, TUNG Brush worked with social media consultant Kristen Matthews and identified twenty-six relevant influencers with presence on blogs and Instagram, across the United States.[8] The brand aimed to engage with a group of influencers but wanted to keep the number manageable so they could have a personal relationship with each influencer. For TUNG Brush, it was important to remain on a personal level with influencers while tracking and knowing where each influencer was on the campaign cycle.

Each influencer was asked to create a blog post and an Instagram post. A key element of the campaign was further engagement on Instagram and building a folio of influencer images they could publish again at a later date. To inspire creativity, TUNG Brush offered a $250 Amazon gift card to the most creative Instagram post. The blog posts ranged from product-specific posts to more organic general posts that highlighted the tongue brush.

The influencers were each sent the ten colors of brushes being considered, along with a link for their followers to vote on the new colors to be added to the range. Each vote required submitting an email address. Voting was encouraged by entering each email address into the drawing for a $250 Amazon gift card. (Influencers were given a unique code for their posts so that TUNG Brush could identify and track the sales from each influencer.)

A large amount of content was created for republication on TUNG Brush's own channel. The data for numbers was not available but a definite increase in sales was reported. The voting link also harvested 5,000 email addresses for the brand's database, adding another level of ROI to the single campaign.

THE DEMING CIRCLE

Almost a decade ago, when I first began developing social media strategies for businesses, there wasn't any framework available to create and measure the effectiveness of one's presence in social media. I had worked in Japan for a number of years and been exposed to the teachings of Professor W. Edwards Deming at a former company.[9] In Japan, Deming is considered the Godfather of Quality Control. He is still revered for his teachings in the 1950s which led to the high-quality, low-cost mass production that helped revolutionize Japan. It's partially through his teachings that companies like Sony and Toyota were able to find success. One of his teachings involved refining processes that can be measured and running the operations through a process called the Deming circle (or Plan, Do, Check, Act [PDCA] circle). Professor Deming adapted and developed the Deming circle from the Shewhart cycle, the work of his own mentor, Walter Shewhart, in order to bring a scientific approach to experiments—but in Japan the same concept was utilized for business.

Figure 10.1 shows how the Deming circle works.

Originally, Deming developed it for quality control and for experiments in production. He was a physicist by trade and saw

THE PDCA CYCLE

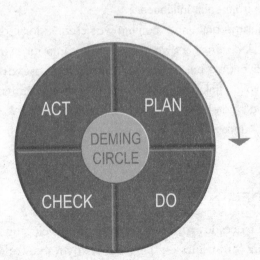

Figure 10.1

the potential benefits of transposing the elements of scientific experimentation to business and production. The circle encourages planning in order to understand what results are wanted before initiating the action, then followed by checking the results and refining them before acting on them and planning the next stage. The cycle continues, encouraging refinement and increased success each time. Since social media is always changing and the Deming Circle is never-ending, I've found that they fit together well to refine results. It's the most appropriate and fitting process for developing social media strategies and influencer marketing programs.

Beginning to build a social media strategy or an influencer program starts in the same place—with the ending in mind. The problem for many social media strategies and influencer marketing programs is that companies don't know how to measure their success. This is new ground and, unlike the traditional marketing landscape, the usual signifiers of a successful campaign are not the same. Often companies embark on engaging influencers in marketing or a social media program without knowing what the signs of success will be. They don't agree on which measuring stick they will use to gauge their efforts, and this leads to constant questioning of their return on investment. If you start with a plan and outline the key performance indicators, then you know from the very start what you will measure and what results mean the work has been a success.

The old saying regarding not measuring a fish by its ability to climb a tree is important to keep in mind when approaching influencer marketing and social media marketing in general. Defining the terms of measurement is essential in understanding how the program is developing. What do you want to achieve? We outline this to start with, then work back to the start, refining the next plan. Then you can define the goals of the program. This allows you to measure and refine the path while developing and adjusting what you're doing to ensure you find the ROI that you're chasing.

WHERE TO START PLANNING YOUR STRATEGY

Start with the end in mind. What return do you want on the investment of time and money? Where do you have strengths and weaknesses compared to your competitors, and which ones are worth developing or improving? What ground do you want to cover by engaging with influencers? To cover these questions, we have to work through several points.

Taking a step back and looking at what is happening on social media with your brand, your industry, and how your competitors measure allows you to understand weaknesses in your brand's approach to social media.

There are a number of tools that businesses should be using to evaluate their digital and social footprint. Before the internet this information was limited and expensive, only available for certain industries in the form of market research reports. While these reports are still relevant, the internet and social media are open frontiers where you can literally spy on the activities of your competitors and easily compare yourselves to them. While you can't glean 100 percent of the information you might like, there is an incredible amount of business intelligence that should serve as benchmarks and competitive KPIs as part of your digital and social efforts.

For instance, monitoring tools on websites like alexa.com give you a rough idea of traffic over different platforms so you can understand how you compare with your competitors. The data shows how you and your competitors fare over different points, allowing you to gain a stronger understanding of the weaknesses in your strategy. Other search engine optimization-specific tools such as SEMrush will actually show you how your search engine rankings compare with your competitors and which keywords and what content drive traffic to their sites. From a social media perspective, data that anyone can access shows the level of fan engagement on any given social network, how much you and your competitors differ on average engagement, and post frequency, along with other points. Running an assessment over recent posts to see where you rank on the social networks that are a critical part of your strategy also gives you a good perspective on how you're faring compared to your competitors. Data points on websites also hint at the strategic importance of their blog and social media presence. Are your competitors proactive and engaging? Is there a strategy?

Other insights you can learn from your competitors' strategies is that perhaps you see they're posting once a day, and far more on Instagram than on Facebook. These insights help you make decisions on what steps to take, where you lead, and what you have to do if you want to challenge in certain ways. Look at the engagement rate and size of community for you and your competitors. Where is the gap? Perhaps you don't want to engage on Instagram or want to allow influencers to do it for you. This is where influencer marketing can help you cover ground. Now you know which areas you want to strategize and prioritize, along with the areas in which you want to use an influencer strategy, paid social strategy, or engage more content marketing.

This information also allows you to refine your target audience and customer. Perhaps your main competitor is aiming at a different demographic than the one you're targeting, and for that reason you have no interest in engaging on the platform they dominate. The more you know and the more you strategize, the more precisely you can target, and the more powerful your influencer marketing engagement can be. You need to know who your audience is and who your customer is. You need to know how they engage on social media and how they engage with you. Which channels are appropriate with your target audience? Millennials are more likely to be engaged through Instagram than Facebook. If you're unable to translate your message to that platform, then find the influencer who can bring your message to your audience there. Gauging and understanding this requires you to listen, so you're better positioned to broadcast your own message to your audience. To do this you need to understand the audience—who is talking, who is the trusted voice, and on what platforms.

Once you have charted the differences between your brand and your competitors', and the ways in which you're engaging on social media, combined with your own internal business and marketing strategies, you have enough background information to begin to define your objectives for your influencer program. Marketing objectives can be divided into two categories—increasing income and decreasing costs. Social media marketing in many ways shares these objectives. In a similar way, these objectives must be clear before implementing the strategy.

Objectives tied to increasing income directly or indirectly are predominantly: increasing brand awareness, building consumer trust and credibility, developing a larger social media community, garnering more engagement for branded content, lead generation and sales, specific product or product-related event promotion, customer retention, search engine optimization through link building, and increased web traffic to fill the funnel. When the objective lies more in decreasing costs, they usually fall into finding ways to use social media for recruiting, customer support, as well as an overall shift away from traditional marketing. Most recently, this also includes the shift of content costs toward influencers in terms of content creation outsourcing. A later section of this chapter will explore some of the more popular objectives in more depth.

A mixture of these objectives is encouraged. Influencer marketing brings a number of intangible benefits as well. These relate to a longer term view of relationship development and support, and include finding new partners, reputation management, customer satisfaction, and empowering advocates. To put things in perspective, Influencer Marketing Hub's 2019 survey of brands engaging in influencer marketing found that most companies were prioritizing objectives around generating brand awareness, increasing sales, or content creation.[10]

Influencer marketing is a process. Defining the objectives early allows you to engage in the process by being able to measure exactly what you need to do for each objective, then work through the Deming circle again, adjust the plan, act accordingly, and put into action the next part of the program. When the objectives are clear, you gain a clearer picture of what is happening when you engage influencers. If you're engaging for one reason but then measuring by another metric or data point, then you will not be able to adjust your strategy accordingly, and you might actually get negative results.

One of the beauties of influencer marketing is that the definition of its success is up to you. Unless you also define the data points of reference, then the results are meaningless. You will not be able to refine the points and then you can't refine what it is that you're doing.

TINY ARMIES

ENGAGING WITH INFLUENCERS WHO SPEAK THE language of your targeted demographic is essential. These influencers have successfully built their own followings on the platforms of their choice because they know how to engage with their audience on those networks. They speak that language and know how to communicate.

To launch their new game Tiny Armies, game developer Play-Stack worked with GameInfluencer. They identified four German mobile game influencers to anchor their campaign.[11] The campaign focused on publicizing the release of the game and encouraging downloads, utilizing the influencers' popularity on YouTube and Twitch. More than just having the influencers show the game off, the campaign was designed around engaging the influencers' followers in a tournament-style battle royale.

PlayStack added a feature to the game specifically for the tournament campaign to help the influencers build their teams. Each influencer founded a team inside the game and on the official game website. Users could then join a team in the game to support their favorite game streamer. The user would collect points while battling other players in the player-vs.-player mode, going toward the influencer's overall score. Building the community was a handy side effect. Involvement and enlistment were incentivized by a series of prizes including a paid trip to Gamescom 2017.

The four influencers launched the campaign on YouTube in their own LetsPlay videos, then live streamed play on Twitch to promote their team and gather their army of users. While the tournament was underway, each influencer published several other shout outs to their communities to encourage involvement while gathering as many players as possible to build their numbers. The final day's play was streamed live, allowing all users and an extended audience to be part of the final part of the tournament as the teams battled for victory.

The results of the campaign were overwhelmingly successful. Data showed that there were 173,530 total views resulting in 9,090 installations of the game. This returned an eCPI (effective cost per installation) of €1.66. The results also showed that the developer experienced a retention rate 14 percent higher than usual.

PLAN OBJECTIVES AND HOW TO MEASURE THEM

Each objective has a corresponding data point, a key performance indicator, or a metric to show the return on investment. These are the most common ones, or the objectives and data points that I've found most effective in my work. This is by no means an exhaustive list. I cannot overemphasize how important it is to be clear about your objectives and how you will measure the data. Once the program is in action, you will get data across a lot of fields. Through this you can compare how different programs work, and the effectiveness of different networks, along with a host of other data metrics. The level of data available can be confusing and overwhelming, and can distract you from your original purpose. However it is essential to stay clear and on point.

You will also have baseline metrics on each influencer and be able to measure them against each other. This can determine who you want to work with going forward and in what way. These data points also provide a baseline when you recruit a new influencer and outline your expected return on investment.

For startups and brands entering new territory, a new industry or sector, or launching a new product, **Increasing Brand Awareness** is often a key objective. Visibility and spread of voice or message through influencers can be an extremely effective way to work toward this. Key indicators to gauge your share of voice and content reach can be measured through social media tools, measuring activity with posts and content shares, along with hashtag engagement.

Often the objective lies in original content or brand messages with the stated aim to **Amplify the Reach and Engagement of Content**. This can be a single piece of content that's shared, or something that's blogged about, mentioned on social media, and discussed. Or it can be defined as ongoing content engagement. This can be measured through content reaction, the number of impressions or clicks, and measuring engagement through social media analytic tools.

Growing Your Social Media Community is especially important for platforms like Instagram where you cannot do a paid follow campaign. On Facebook you can do a campaign to get people to like your page but brands are more limited with Instagram. Obviously, the instant numbers that show whether your community is growing, whether you have more followers or likes, is the immediate indicator here. Taking this one step further, we can also look at comparative measurements. A truer picture will be seen when you look not only at your community but also at the comparative growth rate and engagement rate of your competitors.

Generating Website Traffic or **Generating Leads and Sales** is a common objective, often swinging or adapting the goals of traditional marketing. To measure the effectiveness and the ROI, and level of engagement here, we can use analytic tools to measure the level of referred traffic to your website or to your ecommerce site. There are ways to use special URLs containing UTM parameters to easily measure which influencers are generating the most clicks and traffic and analyze them in web analytics tools such as Google Analytics. Discussion by influencers on social media can be measured through each platform's analytics to see the level of engagement. For a specific gauge on leads and sales, we can measure the effectiveness of each influencer through their codes and discounts.

If your objective is to tie your influencer strategy into your **SEO** efforts, there are analytics to measure the back links from a site to yours. Through social SEO, when people search for your product or a hashtag or similar, they find information about your brand, therefore you can gauge the competitiveness of your content simply by doing searches in the relevant social network and seeing how high your brand ranks.

For many brands it's about a **Shifting Budget from Traditional Marketing** strategy to influencer marketing. The appropriate analytic or point of measurement here would be to look directly at the figures for return on investment. We can compare the ad spend ROI to the influencer spend to see the effectiveness. Measuring and comparing the cost per impression, the cost per click, and the cost per action is easily done using analytical tools, some of which are covered in chapter 13 (the tools chapter) later in this book.

MOCKBERG

HOW DO YOU CONVERT A STRONG FOLLOWING into spending customers? Once you've built a following, perhaps even through influencer campaigns, turning that social media presence into sales often presents a hurdle. Swedish watch brand Mockberg redesigned the buyer's journey, converting followers into sales while broadening their social media reach using only Instagram.

Mockberg realized they were reaching 60,000 followers on Instagram but while their followers had grown, sales hadn't experienced the same upward swing. Working with the Relatable agency, Mockberg recognized that lead generation is driven by a strong incentive—an irresistible, attention-catching hook of an offer. At this point, Mockberg was past the awareness stage of the traditional buyer's journey. Anchoring the campaign to Mockberg's 60,000 followers, they established a giveaway offer.[12]

After becoming aware of your brand, and by following you, users are certainly aware of what you do, but they need a reason to act and buy your product—identified by Relatable and Mockberg as an irresistible offer with real scarcity and urgency, followed by a clear call to action. In this case, Mockberg offered vouchers of €60, having users share their email addresses and tag a friend for a chance to win one of the sixty vouchers. Mockberg was able to capture the emails in the comments, saving the new emails in real time and making a personalized offer to each lead. This expanded the way Mockberg could reach their fans by creating a new platform for contact, and another way to turn them into customers.

Within a week Mockberg generated 326 new leads backed with data that showed that 30 percent of users who interacted with the post participated in the campaign. The post in the campaign generated $7,406 in revenue and 1,117 interactions.

On top of using their own Instagram to reach out, Mockberg enlisted the help of influencers. Working with an agency, Mockberg identified a small but highly relevant group of fashion influencers, focusing on their level of reach and engagement. Seven influencers were brought on board as brand ambassadors, expanding the reach of the campaign to more than a million further Instagram users. At the end of the campaign Mockberg had reached 1,010,078 followers by collaborating with the seven fashion influencers who each posted the link once. The seven posts received

23,452 likes, comments, and mentions in total, generating 1,363 new leads. The campaign generated $13,061 in revenue. This new channel projected $100,000 in extra revenue over the next year.

STRATEGIZING THROUGH EXCLUSION

One of the key elements of strategy that is so often overlooked is deciding what *not* to do. You don't have to be everywhere. Social media is so broad now that it's practically impossible to be everywhere. And trying to do so actually hurts your efforts. Engaging on Snapchat or Twitch when you're a B2B office equipment firm takes away from your key message and misses the demographic completely. If you have a profile on a medium that you don't use or don't know how to engage with effectively, then it's detrimental to your overall strategy. When people search for your brand you don't want them to find a dormant account with few followers. Every interaction with your brand is an opportunity to add to your image or lose prestige. Deciding what not to engage in and what to *not* do is as important a decision as what you will do. It will help you refine strategy and decide how to build on your strengths.

This is also where influencers can do the work for you and cover ground that you can't reach or with which you are unfamiliar. Perhaps you don't know how to best communicate through YouTube, or you have difficulty communicating visually through Instagram. Engaging with influencers who know how to communicate through these platforms benefits your brand and message more than running blindly into the fray. Integrating influencers into your entire social media program to help your weaker parts is part of a coherent strategy. Engaging and developing your social media and influencer strategy does not mean that you have to do everything. It's about choosing and prioritizing what is important, then using this information to strategize.

SALVATION ARMY

NONPROFITS CAN ALSO BENEFIT FROM THE tools influencers bring to the table to spread their message and create awareness.

The Salvation Army engaged an agency to work with influencers during a recent Red Kettle season campaign. The program utilized several influencers, harnessing them as brand ambassadors, involving them in fundraising efforts, and leveraging the influencers' social media followings for further recognition and publicity. However, it was the results from influencer Chris Strub that stood out the most.

The #FightForGoodTour put Chris on the road for over a month.[13] He traveled through twenty-five of the eastern United States, interacting with the local community, helping out at Salvation Army–operated charities and collecting money, while documenting the experience. Chris was one of a handful of influencers who worked with the Salvation Army during these weeks to raise awareness of the charity's efforts leading up to Christmas. The influencers used their network to spread the news and information about what was happening and the multifaceted approach of the Salvation Army.

Chris posted all the content about his travels on various social media accounts. He created videos and shared the experience of meeting those who benefit from the Salvation Army's work. The Salvation Army allowed Chris to document his travels however he wanted, allowing his organic voice to spread the message. These included Instagram story takeovers, Facebook Live events, and videos on his own personal channels with the appropriate hashtags.

Across Facebook and YouTube, the video series was viewed a total of 14,200 times, The Instagram Stories received 24,276 impressions, while the Instagram grid received 39,605 impressions. Based on average views, the campaign brought around 25,000 Snapchat impressions. Over the course of the campaign, Chris's 1,676 Tweets had a total of 885,245 impressions and 16,378 engagements, including 1,566 retweets. When looking at the entire Salvation Army Red Kettle season period at the end of December, the total tweet impressions for @ChrisStrub exceeded 1 million. The campaign to raise awareness, along with the fundraising drive, was considered a success.

THE ART AND SCIENCE OF
INFLUENCER IDENTIFICATION

The biggest challenge for many in influencer marketing remains finding the right influencer to partner with in the first place. The second biggest is finding ways to engage in a mutually beneficial relationship. The work in preparation is key. Part of this challenge is changing everyone's mind-set to understand that it's a relationship, it's a collaboration and not a transaction. Working with an influencer involves a different level of engagement, and a different investment to develop the relationship. Just as with all long-term relationships, investments and demands are different. It takes time to understand each other's wants and needs. It takes time to understand what you need to give to turn an influencer into an advocate for your brand.

At this point, now that social media marketing is mainstream and most brands have at least considered influencer marketing, many have begun to realize that influence does not necessarily have a linear correlation to the size of one's community. It is more realistically about reach and engagement on posts. As discussed earlier, influencers with a moderate number of followers often have higher engagement. When you're targeting a particular demographic or perhaps reaching out to a different demographic with a new launch or product, engaging micro-influencers or a niche following can be far more effective in achieving your goals than working with an influencer with millions of followers. Working with five influencers who have ten thousand followers each might give better reach and engagement than one person with a hundred thousand followers.

All of this makes finding the right influencer(s) to work with both more challenging and more critical to the success of your influencer marketing program. Furthermore, the influencer must be aligned with the objectives of your program.

THE LAY OF THE LAND

Influencers come from a variety of backgrounds. They create content in different ways and wield different kinds of influence. Considering who they speak to is essential. I am reminded of the story of a brand working with a female bodybuilder to promote their line of sporting clothes for women. Had they done research they would have found out that an overwhelming majority of the influencer's followers were men, not the female fitness enthusiasts the brand had intended to reach. In the same vein, if a brand has worked to establish "street cred" then engaging with an influencer who doesn't fit that core value and image will work against the groundwork already laid. Perhaps the brand will lose credibility with the core demographic. Perhaps it will strengthen the brand's hold. These are essential questions to address in assessing the lay of the land before looking at the influencers. So what community do you want to engage? Who is the target audience? Who are they listening to? Once that is clear, we map. A lot.

Some influencer programs start by creating a pool of tens or hundreds of influencers and seeing who fits the core values and brand affinity best. Some cases I've heard of started by mapping a few thousand influencers. This might seem like an extreme number, but with influencers existing in any given community with a wide range of community sizes, the numbers of influencers will only continue to grow. Although you're not cold calling these people to sell your brand, the idea of playing percentages is similar. You want to start with a number much larger than those with whom you will develop a relationship.

CLIF KID

WHEN MAPPING YOUR COMMUNITY, IT CAN SEEM like there are too many influencers to engage with on a small scale. You can start small and scale up, or you can aim for a large program at the very beginning. How do you begin looking at a campaign on such a level? What benefits does going big bring?

When CLIF Kid looked to spread the message about their organic and nutritious snacks for children, they decided to start big. The brand worked with an agency to map their community and the target markets.[1] In this case it was engaging with parents and promoting the message that children need to be active outside of the classroom, reinforcing the brand values of nutrition and organic food.

Part of the campaign was to ensure the message was visible everywhere for parents. The brand engaged influencers with parent-friendly audiences. The engagement was spread across several platforms in different levels including a blog program, Instagram engagement, amplification, content seeding, Twitter party, and syndication.

The campaign involved more than six hundred influencers. The multiple levels to the campaign, along with the numbers, really puts this campaign in a larger field than many of the other case studies I've included in this book. Such an undertaking would take a lot more energy and time investment to manage than a smaller campaign but sometimes going big is the right approach. Ensuring the message is everywhere and being able to amplify the content of six hundred influencers means you have a lot of options across multiple platforms.

The campaign resulted in 565.5 million impressions of branded content, over 301,000 views of the YouTube video, and more than 79,000 engagements on Instagram—marking a 4.1 percent engagement rate for the brand.

This approach deals with numbers on a scale similar to running a traditional advertising slot. A show such as *The Big Bang Theory* draws roughly 20 million viewers per episode.[2] With this many impressions for their influencer campaign, CLIF Kid took that large scale to social media, engaging eyeballs at a rate higher than a traditional television commercial campaign during a peak-hour sitcom.

Start by knowing who you're searching for influencer-wise. Influencers are simply people around us who have built a platform on social media and are trusted by their audience. They could be customers who already have brand affinity. They could be followers or advocates who are already sharing your brand's posts and engaging. They already have brand affinity and, for this reason, it's easy to turn them into influencers. Similarly, they may be people already talking about your product or about something similar in the industry. They are already involved with the conversation, so turning their voices into influencing for your brand is the ideal next step.

To explore the options here from an extremely holistic perspective, we can conduct searches for keywords and hashtags across the platforms with which you want to engage just as an average social media user who is looking for information would. We see the landscape and the scope of the discussions and conversations. It really is a matter of fitting into the discussions that are happening. It can't look like advertising, since influencer marketing does not play by those rules. If you approached an influencer with that angle, and they were foolish enough to take on your message, then it would ruin both your credibility and theirs. It is easy to spot an ad and easy to identify a message that is disingenuous. Instead, we see what discussions and conversations are there, and pinpoint what is being talked about. We look at how that topic can become about your brand or product and take stock of the voices who are best able to deliver that message. If they're already talking about your brand, or about your competitors, then they are already covering the demographic. Once you have a list of influencers already involved in the discussion, list them by brand affinity from greatest to least.

When W Hotels began looking for an influencer they decided to first look through their 165,000 Instagram followers.[3] One of their followers was a photographer with a strong following, a regular poster of new content who traveled a lot. This was ideal. He was able to produce content that worked visually, while already covering the demographic of travelers who stay at W Hotels. On top of that, he already followed and shared the hotel content, so brand affinity was established. Reaching out to him proved fruitful and beneficial for both parties so they took their relationship to the next level.

THE METHOD TO THE MADNESS

You can do a large amount of work offline. Much of this work can be done manually without tools. Doing so presents an advantage I'll soon explain. Offline methods include asking people around you who they listen to and who influences them. Are these influencers already talking about similar products? How is the reaction to their posts? Do they talk about many products in your market, or only one?

To start, ask anyone. Employees, salespeople, partners, marketers, customers, and anyone else around you and your brand. Anyone can be active on social media. Anyone can have a hand in online conversations. Learning who to ask is part of this early procedure. There are many influencers who you have never heard of, and for this reason it's important to look at the demographic you want to reach and then walk back your search from these results. Your kids and the children of your employees or neighbors might have a better understanding of who is being listened to if they fit the demographic you want to reach. Asking them who influences them is essential to understanding the landscape before launching your program.

Looking at customer decisions is another easy indicator. Did they make a decision because of an influencer? Who do your customers already listen to? This can lead to discovering influencers who already have an affinity for your brand, and who are already talking positively about your product.

After working through the offline methods, turning to online methods for recommendations and searches gives you an understanding of the depth of influencers. Following up the offline elements with online research gives you a chance to see the overlap. Obvious places to start are in Google searches to find the relevant posts or articles posted by influencers. Looking for bloggers or Instagrammers, Twitter voices, and so on with the relevant keywords gives you a quick overview of who is out there. This will also lead you to roundup posts and other top-ten lists of who is active in your industry. On social media it's easy enough to look through Facebook for posts or search Instagram hashtags specific to your brand, industry, or product. LinkedIn allows keyword searches to reveal who is active there. Twitter users can curate lists on a variety of topics, and this works in your favor. After you look through a few of these lists already curated for your convenience, you will see patterns and trends on who is influencing and who is being listened to. From these you can search further and see who is engaging with their audience, and on what level. This will inevitably show you other influencers and other voices, other hashtags and discussions that demonstrate further voices on your topic.

It's important to remember that in an entire ocean of influencers, you're not randomly looking for someone. You're not just looking for the first influencer to leap out of the big blue. You're looking for someone who connects with you in a whole other way. To make the search as efficient as possible, you need to make the characteristics as defined as possible. The location, the audience, the level of engagement, the topics that they usually post about, the frequency of posts, the content media that they prefer—these are all aspects to consider when defining just who it is you're looking for. The more specific identifiers you can pinpoint, the easier it is to know what you're looking for in the first place. All of this will filter out the crowd to find your perfect match.

Bumble Bee food company was looking for a brand ambassador.[4] The brand approached an agency to help them partner with an influencer for a long-term relationship. They identified their needs and their values. They were looking for a long-term relationship with a fitness influencer. The brand specifically wanted to work with a single influencer located in the United States who aligned with the core values of the company. On top of this, they wanted someone who posted quality content on fitness with credibility through fitness trainer credentials. The agency created a pool and sorted through the characteristics to find the perfect partnership. Now Presley Salmon, a fitness blogger who matched the entire list of characteristics, has produced more than a hundred pieces of content in a long-term relationship.

LEESA

LEESA SELLS LUXURY MATTRESSES DIRECT TO THE customer without a showroom. Investing in something as essential to your lifestyle as a mattress without being able to test it takes a large leap of faith. Leesa offers a one-hundred-day return on their mattresses but the initial investment in a luxury mattress still asks a lot of potential customers. The brand knew this and looked to influencer marketing as a way to both spread product knowledge and inspire trust in the company.[5]

The original brief started small. Leesa wanted to reach an online-savvy female audience who was interested in buying a mattress and looking to purchase in the next six months. They targeted a small range of bloggers who were identified as expert reviewers for ecommerce brands. Leesa gifted a mattress in exchange for an unbiased review. The bloggers were selected on their strength with the desired demographic as well as their authentic voice. Leesa was not the only brand to do this, and some blogs took it upon themselves to compare the different mattresses. The blogs also began including unboxing videos. By spreading information about their mattresses, the reviews and comparisons, and the excitement of the unboxing videos, potential customers were given a great deal of information about what to expect when buying a Leesa mattress.

The brand saw what was working and looked for how to scale the process. The first step was to see what kind of content created the best engagement and then to expand the reach. The most effective content was the personal testimonials and the unboxing videos. Leesa expanded the influencers and bloggers to those with influence in DIY and style, including interior design. High engagement and the style of voice were key factors in deciding who to work with.

By engaging with those influencers posting with an authentic voice, Leesa was able to drive over 100,000 clicks to the website, resulting in more than four hundred sales in the period recorded. The extra online presence and strength of voice also proved positive as a long-lasting beneficial side effect.

HUNTER GATHERER TOOLS

There is an increasingly large number of tools online to help you identify and scale your influencer program, but what I suggest is starting without them and doing the work manually. This advice might sound counterintuitive to a digital marketer that relies on tools to measure and optimize, but I have my reasoning. The sheer range of tools can be overwhelming and give you results that, if you haven't properly decided what you're looking for, can be confusing. When you know what you're looking for then a tool is useful. But using a tool just because it's there is inefficient. A spirit level is useful when hanging a picture on a wall to ensure the frame is straight, but if all you need is to bang the nail into the wall then a spirit level is not going to give you the best results. Using a hammer to measure if the frame is straight will also be a waste of time. The concept correlates with online tools. Understanding what you want to measure and which tool is most useful saves time and energy, and therefore money, as well as produces clearer results.

Many marketers jump to tools. It's understandable: Tools are there to make life easier. But starting with manual identification is helpful for many reasons. For my money, beginning without tools allows you to understand the social user's perspective more deeply from the initial step into the pool. A tool might identify a handful of influencers that tick the right metrics for the search but that, for some reason, users don't find when searching the right keywords. Potential customers, the clients, and the demographic you want to reach through influencers do not use these tools or follow these metrics to find the information they're after. They search through Google. They read Facebook and Twitter posts. They look for hashtags on Instagram. If the social media user you want to reach uses this method to find the information you want to put out, then you should use the same methods to see who they find when they do these searches.

How do your potential community and your future customers find this information? Who do they listen to? When you investigate these ways and follow the hashtags and blog posts through to the source, then you understand what your customer is doing to find the information. This gives you understanding of the new buyer's journey through the web. This gives you clearer understanding of what is being read and who is producing the content that is influencing your audience.

The list of influencers you gather from this exercise is not a Rolodex to run through. Mass emailing them won't get them to support your brand or cause. They are people to connect with and to partner with to go forward. Starting with offline methods, I find, gives you a more natural and intuitive approach to begin. Connecting through organic and manual methods also helps when assessing visual social media. Just looking at a potential partner's feed can cover data points that a tool won't find—both positive and negative. This allows you to better measure influencers' alignment with your brand identity and core values.

Onalytica, a company specializing in digital tools for identifying influencers, together with the agency Formative, took a challenge to compare the two approaches to identifying influencers.[6] The two agencies were given the same brief for the same client. Onalytica set about analyzing data and metrics, ran the pool of influencers through the filters to find what the client had specified, and found 294 potential influencers with whom the client could engage. Formative took the information and list of characteristics from the client and ran a manual approach, looking through organic methods. They found a pool of 364 influencers. The search was admittedly not as extensive as it could have been—a light search focusing on creating a pool rather than thinning out the possible influencers. The interesting result in this exercise is that only 39 influencers were identified by both agencies. That's a remarkably low percentage. The two processes returned very different results, and largely different pools of influencers. Rather than show the different strengths, the case study shows the worth of investigating in more than one way. Manual and online tool strategies identify different aspects of influencers. More examination would discover if the 39 overlapping results were actually the best influencers for the client's program, but even after adopting tools, this type of hybrid approach is recommended to ensure that you leave no stone unturned.

This isn't to say that tools can't play a role in influencer identification. Tools access different APIs (application programing interface) and process data in minutes that would take a human years to do, and often in error. They uncover insights that the manual processes can't see. The manual approach is deeply contextual and often costs very little. The tools might give a richer data set, and this is especially useful in looking at changing influence over time. Tools also provide insights from data manipulation. However, I would argue that manual should be done first. You will look manually at the influencers identified by the tools anyway. I agree both have their place but undertaking the manual identification first gives you an initial organic approach that will benefit you later when connecting with influencers. The hybrid approach covers both perspectives.

HAWAII TOURISM BUREAU

LAUNCHING A HASHTAG AND HOPING FOR ENgagement is one thing, but to get it to take off is another. How can you engage user-generated content with your hashtag in an efficient way? How can you plant the seeds for the hashtag to continue to create attention after the launch? Identifying a leveraging point and key influencers is the starting point.

Instagram has become the default place for visual communication. The visual element of the medium, and the way that key influencers have harnessed the power of communicating visually, means that Instagram lends itself to visual communication and influencer campaigns remarkably well. When you have a product or location that lends itself to visual representation, the challenge then becomes to ensure you're publishing content that people haven't seen.

The Hawaii Tourism Board turned to Instagram to launch a campaign which, while dated, still shows the growing power that Instagram has for the travel industry.[7] At the core of the campaign was the idea of bringing somewhat unique images of Hawaii to social networks so that users could see them and believe that they, too, could have an experience like the one covered in the post. To do this, the campaign was to involve as much user-generated content as possible and amplify the hashtag through engaging with high-profile travel influencers. The Hawaii Visitors and Conventions Bureau engaged popular travel Instagrammers including Jordan Hershel, who brought a reputation for chasing off-the-beaten-path type travel destinations. Engaging with these travel influencers popularized the hashtag. The bureau also engaged prominent Hawaiian ambassadors such as the former Miss Hawaii, popular lifestyle bloggers, and surfer/photographers with a local touch.

The campaign brought much attention to the islands. In the following months, almost 100,000 posts used the hashtag, including both user-generated content and sponsored Instagram posts. The campaign reached over half of all U.S. travelers through various social media and paid avenues, resulting in a response that indicated over two-thirds of them planned to visit the Hawaiian Islands during an upcoming vacation.

AUDITING AND RANKING INFLUENCERS

The recent ACTIVATE State of Influencer Marketing Study provides some important data regarding the key points marketers look for when vetting influencers for campaigns. These five key points were chosen by a majority of marketers surveyed:

Quality of Content—Along with which I would include the authenticity, relevance, and frequency of publishing.

Engagement Rates—Ensuring the content was being reacted to in the desired way.

Audience Demographics—Which I would assume includes relevance, size, and choice of social network.

Pre-Existing Brand Affinity—Has the influencer tagged your brand in their photos or spoken about it in social media?

Past Brand Partnerships—Have they already engaged with and been vetted by similar brands and were their posts successful?

There are many different ways to evaluate an influencer with the above as one guide. Missteps often occur when applying the same approach as other campaigns. There is an inherent organic side to working with an influencer. It's not as transactional as considering the publication in which to run an advertising campaign.

Expanding upon the above data, I recommend my clients to additionally take all of the following into account when identifying which influencer(s) to work with:

Relevance—While it was hinted at in Quality of Content, does the relevance of the influencer's content match that of your demographic? Remember that anecdote of the female fitness model who had a predominantly male following, meaning that although the images might match a female clothing brand, it would be irrelevant to engage this influencer.

SEO/Viral Value—Does the post come up on Google or YouTube if you search for it? Will the content have a life after the initial posting? This also includes where the content appears in search results within a given social network such as on Instagram.

Personality—Does it align with your corporate identity? Does it fit with your brand message? Are there any red flags to consider?

Advertising Frequency—If every other influencer post is an #ad, it brings to question how much authentic engagement you will receive from collaborating with them.

What you want out of an influencer relationship will vary brand by brand. It may even vary for your own needs from influencer to influencer, or for the changing emphasis of your program over time. For this reason, it's important to put your own weight on each point of this audit. The elements or details that you place importance on are unique for your needs. Perhaps relevance and audience are more important for your brand than established brand affinity. Or perhaps you're looking for personality and fit more than anything in order to establish a long-term relationship. Place your own weighted score for each of these points similar to a social media audit.

Once you've narrowed down the field of potential influencers to connect with, it's important to return to the fundamental question: If an influencer shared your message, would it align and resonate with their community? This is the heart of the matter that you want to address before going any further, before becoming involved in the marriage with an influencer. If you want to work with an influencer but they don't post what you want them to post about, your message probably won't resonate with their community. The message won't have any impact, and that's the key measure. You don't want to work with an influencer, who, after they post about your brand, end up having comments like, "Your photo looks like a blatant advertisement." Of course, most users who find out-of-place sponsored content won't bother leaving such a comment; they simply will not engage with that content, lowering its overall engagement performance.

When you've built this pool to draw from then you have the base of potential relationships to explore. With the pool at your fingertips, you can explore the essential question with a range of influencers and see who has the potential to engage with you in the way you want. Which influencers in this pool would have the most resonance with their followers if they shared your content? Which of them actually want to engage you in a conversation and brainstorm ways in which you might build a mutually beneficial relationship?

It's a smart idea to run through the audit, at least on some level, every quarter or six months. It's not necessarily worth going in depth each time but the point is to stay on top of emerging influencers and changing voices. Some tools have an embedded function to keep you up to date and help you stay on top of the changing landscape.

12

CREATING AND MANAGING
INFLUENCER RELATIONSHIPS

After working through the identification process, you'll have a pool of influencers you want to work with. These are the ones to begin to create a relationship with. Focus on them.

Like sales, creating relationships with influencers is a percentage game. Not everyone you want to engage with will do so. Not everyone you reach out to will fit. Sometimes the timing isn't right for whatever reason. From the pool you have, you will convert some of these influencers to advocates. Some you won't.

SENDING SOCIAL SIGNALS

First you have to qualify with the influencer. You have to let them know that you're aware of what they're doing, and that you're into it. It's a bit like dating. Eventually you reach out to them to gauge mutual interest. It's the first contact. First impressions count.

A social signal is any action you perform on social media that will result in your name appearing in the notifications of the person you are engaging with. It could be as simple as a follow or like of their content or as deep as a comment or repost of their image. Influencers look at the engagement they receive from their community, so you would hope to be noticed if you engage with them.

IT'S A NUMBERS GAME

Not all will engage back with you, but some will. These are the ones you contact in the next stage when you reach out via email or otherwise. Not all of these influencers will want to work with your brand. When negotiating the terms of the partnership there will be another percentage who don't click with you. Being relevant and influential yourself as a brand gives you an edge here too: Given a choice, influencers will want to work with a well-known brand. It gives the influencer credibility and helps their resume to be able to say they've worked with large brands. If you're a smaller brand then the respondent pool might be lower and a different kind of work will have to be done. This is where existing brand affinity goes a long way at the start of the relationships for smaller brands. Building your own influence is essential on more than one level, and in this case it can shortcut some of the introduction. (This will be covered in more depth in Part Four.)

THE FUNNEL

The framework in developing relationships with influencers and converting them into brand advocates can be viewed as an eight-step process (see Figure 12.1). It's a funnel of engagement.

THE INFLUENCER ENGAGEMENT FUNNEL

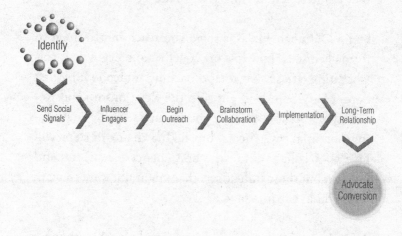

Figure 12.1

At certain points there will be a way to gauge who fits you best. There will be points where influencers, or even you, will decide that you're not compatible. The process will not go further with that influencer and it's not a bad thing; why continue with someone who wants different things? Move your energy elsewhere.

Identify—This is the process covered in the all of chapter 11. It means finding the pool of influencers who you wish to engage.

Send Social Signals—Working with the power of social networks, you begin to form a relationship and engage with the influencers, sending social signals, just as social media users would.

Influencer Engages—This stage is up to the influencer. After engaging through social networks, they follow you back, send you comments, or react in a way that shows they're interested in what your brand does.

Begin Outreach—In this stage you reach out to them to formally discuss how to work together and begin your collaboration. It's similar to approaching someone for a first date. Many brands might skip the Relationship and Response phases and directly go to Outreach after identifying potential influencers, but taking the extra steps will give your collaboration the best chance for success and help vet out those influencers that might not want to work with you in the first place.

Brainstorm Collaboration—Like any relationship, there's a stage where both parties decide that there is a mutual benefit and the partnership should continue. At this point, you establish what you both want. The "official" relationship begins.

Implementation—Where the influencer actually implements the agreed-upon action. While there is incredible work involved up until this point, it's important to remember that you need to validate that the influencer has done as promised, especially if there is a commercial arrangement involved. Believe it or not, there have been lawsuits regarding influencers who failed to influence according to their arrangement.[1]

Long-term Relationship—After the first campaign you explore the future. Is there possibility for more work? In what ways will you collaborate again? You discuss the details of how to go forward.

Advocate Conversion—Once a long-term relationship has been entered into, you turn the relationship into brand advocacy. A sign of this is when the influencer begins to talk about you or recommend you even though you have not asked them to do so as part of your arrangement.

This process takes time. It's not necessarily straightforward. In other models or frameworks around marketing there is often a time frame attached to each action point and a sign of when each element is being executed. Not here. You're building real relationships with real people. You cannot make demands like other forms of marketing, and you cannot approach an influencer like they're a digital content creation machine. It will take time, but the results will impress.

GNC

ONLINE CONVERSATIONS HAPPEN EVERYWHERE in social media, not just on Instagram.

When GNC was exploring ways to engage with influencers they realized the power social media brings in being able to open communication.[2] As a health food and health lifestyle brand, GNC recognized parts of their demographic had not been engaged. The niche area of GNC's clientele communicates widely on internet forums. Engaging a brand-wide campaign would still miss these sectors. But opening conversations individually and engaging the influencers in each niche could open dialogue.

The brand realized that many newcomers to the field of health and bodybuilding sought answers on these forums. However, the jargon and tone of much of the advice wasn't welcoming and informative to beginners. GNC engaged influential voices and encouraged more informative discussion. The campaign was backed with traditional influencer approaches such as gifting product in return for published reviews.

The same approach was used to find the niche groups discussing areas where GNC products would fit but the people weren't necessarily exposed to the brand. This included yoga and women's fitness areas who had perhaps dismissed GNC by traditionally linking the brand with male bodybuilding supplements.

Over several months, GNC noted that influencer involvement brought more than 383,000 fans on Facebook and 60,000 followers on Twitter. The brand also noted that there was significantly higher traffic to the online store from social media networks. The results were impressive enough that the marketing campaign planned more involvement at this grassroots level for the next calendar year to build on the organic engagement.

WHY WOULD INFLUENCERS WORK WITH YOU?

Understanding what you can bring to the table begins by understanding just what motivates influencers. A CrowdTap study showed that, outside of money, a whopping 75 percent of influencers were motivated by either having an opportunity that was relevant to their audience, being able to give a unique experience to their audience, or simply that they liked a brand.[3] Another study by TapInfluence revealed that the number-one factor influencers consider when approached by a brand is alignment with the brand's core values and only 11 percent said that payment was the most important factor.[4] Perhaps they want unique product access or discounts for their community. Perhaps they want a shout out or a promotion on your channels. Perhaps you have the ability to open doors and make introductions that can help them. Perhaps they want increased traffic on their channels and networks. By doing the research involved with identifying influencers, you will ensure that the opportunity is relevant to their audience. Interestingly enough, the third most common response in the CrowdTap study—that they liked the brand—shows how powerful existing affinity is: another element covered in your groundwork for identifying influencers.

A separate study by VentureBeat showed that 72 percent of influencers responded that inadequate compensation is the biggest mistake made by brands when starting to work together.[5] This is often the difference between a social celebrity and an everyday influencer. Approaching a social celebrity for a shout out on their social media, or to use your product, comes with the inferred understanding that there's a fee. There is a more transactional nature to the approach. They are a celebrity, of sorts, and so they run their social media accounts as a business. The flipside of this is that it might lead you to undercut the micro-influencer by thinking that they would be flattered to be approached and that a $20 Amazon gift card would suffice. The mistake here is not having the conversation that you need to have.

There is a pyramid-type shape to influencers and followers, with a few at the top with millions of followers, and increasing numbers as the audiences get smaller. Where micro-influencers can have an advantage is that they have a higher engagement rate with their audiences. This is why the process of identification is so important. Becoming involved with an influencer who is still at the micro-influencer level also gives you the chance to work with them while they grow.

The influencer marketing platform company Klear (https://klear.com) has published an Influencer Marketing Rate Card which states that those with followers in the range of 500 to 500,000 charge between $100 and $507 per Instagram post. This gives you a general feel for the baseline of the financial aspect of engagement. Some influencers list their rates on their sites or profiles. Shoutcart, another site used to engage with influencers, lists influencers and shout outs with the price, the deals and conditions on the post, and the amount of time the post will be kept visible. At this point, it's worth comparing these costs with your own paid social costs and the return on your own spend. Ideally, they are complementary.

Influencers can bring incredible value for a potentially small investment. I was invited to attend an Adobe Summit in Las Vegas along with a number of influencers.[6] I wasn't paid for the conference, per se, but the travel expenses were covered by the brand. We received exclusive access and content that we were able to share with our networks. We were able to interview people in the company and produce our own content. At no cost to Adobe, we told the story of the event through tweets and Instagram posts. A *Forbes* article about the event revealed that the top nine influencers there generated more than 227 million impressions for the summit. In advertising costs, taking an eCPM of $20, this reach would have cost $4.6 million. Beyond just that, value was added to this information simply through the fact that the news came from trusted people with interested audiences who were already predisposed toward the information, not just advertising or self-promotion from Adobe. The information was presented by influencers in ways that they knew would engage with their audiences, making Adobe look good in the process. That is a huge amount of promotion and value for very little spend. Understanding this potential is key to maximizing your engagement of influencers.

Lastly, concerning budget, consider that different media require different things. A 500-word blog post is different from a

2,000-word one. Producing a ten-second video differs from five minutes. YouTube, Facebook, and Instagram content options all have different demands on the influencer's time and intellectual property.

BUILD THE RELATIONSHIP FIRST

Start by engaging with your identified influencer on their preferred social network. Follow them. Look through their content and share it. Engage through relevant comments. This is the step to take to see if they will reciprocate the attention. It's sending social signals, then seeing how they react to you reaching out to them.

Brands often don't realize just how much they can connect with influencers on social media. Part of the confusion is over the difference between profiles and accounts. There are two kinds of social networks. The first are those where a brand or company creates a company profile. These include Facebook and LinkedIn. It's a pay-to-play scenario, and because of this it's difficult to get any organic interaction. The algorithms heavily favor people, and brands struggle. The second kind are those with accounts where the experience is more or less the same if you're a brand or a person. These include YouTube, Twitter, Pinterest, and Instagram. The way these networks are set up allows different types of interactions. While we can't follow people on our Facebook page, we can use a brand account to follow people and influencers on Instagram. We can retweet or follow in Twitter. We can comment on posts. Our engagement can be much more proactive. It's because of these possibilities and the way these networks function that causes brands to shift efforts to Twitter or Instagram. When working in B2B environments, Twitter is essential for building rapport and sending social signals to the influencers you've identified because of the limitations LinkedIn puts on company pages.

At this point, it's important to think about a long-term plan. The benefit of having it already devised is that the questions you address then will be asked by influencers later. If the decisions have already been addressed, then you're ahead of the game. Once you've developed a pool of influencers you can work with for a variety of situations, you can begin looking at short-term goals. The points you cover in devising a longer term strategy will be the basis of the agreement you come to with the influencer, so thinking about it beforehand can save time.

These points include:

Background information about your company, including strategy, why you have this program, and why you want to work with influencers

Deliverables, and what you expect from influencers you engage with in terms of content or posts

Calls to action and other elements including hashtags and strategic links

Creative elements from the influencer including images, and which networks you want them posted to

Timing and frequency, including when you want certain hashtags or images to begin circulating, and how many times a week or month you want the influencer to mention it

Think of these things before having the conversation with influencers so you can move rapidly when the influencer indicates she is on board.

THE U.S. FEDERAL TRADE COMMISSION, AND MANY other government departments globally, have introduced guidelines to protect consumers from misleading content. Essentially it comes down to: If you're being paid for talking about a product then there are guidelines about endorsement. Beginning in September 2017, the FTC contacted brands and influencers with warnings about their content.[7] The general FTC guidelines indicate that any sponsored or paid content should be clearly marked on the post, not on a click-through link. Any non-monetary sponsorship arrangements should also be mentioned. The sponsorship disclosure should be hard to miss and not ambiguous through hashtags like #collab, #thanks, or #spon. Laws are changing globally, and it's the responsibility of both brands and influencers to ensure their work remains on the right side of the law. For this reason you should check with the requirements of the relevant commissions in the regions where you're operating.

THE OUTREACH

The power of influencer marketing lies in the human and personal nature of how influencers communicate. The initial connection and engagement with influencers is the same—it's human. You have to contact them personally. Some tools grab email addresses and can send out blanket emails, but this often ends up as spam. Sometimes the email address is out of date or irrelevant. It's impersonal. Connecting with an influencer after they've returned your initial interaction involves looking at their profile and finding their contact details. It's more than likely they have contact information there, along with their preferred method of interacting with you. They are influencers. They want brands to contact them.

The message must be personalized. There are many tools that have increased the ability to connect with many people with a short investment of time, either through email or otherwise. To garner the support of the influencer, you have to work in the opposite direction and invest the time for just one contact. The entire reason you're contacting them is because you think they will be important for your company for a long time going forward. So it's important to invest the time in a personal message.

Influencers are often contacted by several different companies. That's the nature of their position. It's important to follow the contact advice on their Instagram profile, other social media profile, or website. You have already made some connection on social media and sent the social signals. Following up with an email is an extension of this. Hashoff published a study called "State of the Union" which showed that of the influencers they interviewed, 35 percent work full time, 25 percent were students, and another 22 percent work part time.[8] Many of them could be classified as a one-person startup or solopreneur. They're busy. If you frame your communication to them in the way they've suggested, then you make it easy for them, and they might be more willing to reply.

If the influencer prefers you to DM them (send them a Direct Message through that particular social network), then you should be more conversational but to the point. An example DM might read: "Neal, we love your content and would love to collaborate. If interested let me know the best email or phone number to reach you at." DMs are meant for shorter conversations, so it just might be the perfect medium for you to begin the outreach. Don't overthink it. Keep it as simple and straightforward as users using DMs would.

Outreach by email, even if you know their email address from their response or profile, creates a larger challenge because you're already competing for their attention with all of the other emails they receive. First, a clear subject line that makes them want to open the email is essential. This may take some testing, but it must feel personalized.

The purpose of the email must also be clear and personal. Explain how you found them and why you're reaching out to them. The email must contain genuine praise and respect for their work as well. It must be authentic. With the early work done, they already know that your brand liked or shared the content. Following up those posts with this email ensures the praise is authentic. Why did certain posts resonate with your brand? Point out any specific content that you found enlightening or that has cultural affinity to your brand. These are points that you highlighted in the process of influencer identification. These are the things that made them stand out in the first place, so you should already have examples at hand.

Finding common points of connection is another way to instantly personalize the communication. Find any common friends or colleagues through their profile. Perhaps you can see they attended your alma mater on their LinkedIn profile. It's a transaction and like any other social transaction, you want to underline common elements. Investing time early in the process in personalizing the message can go a long way later.

Inspire interest in their mind by highlighting the value you can provide them. What is in it for the influencer? This is the benefit you want to highlight and show them, along with demonstrating your track record and the work you've done with influencers in the past. It's a sale but it's also a proposal of a partnership. Showing that you understand this is a good sign that you know what you're doing. Showing that you under-stand how collaborating with influencers works inspires trust and leads to the next step, which is when they respond. Having a clear next step allows them to answer easily. Perhaps you want to set up a call. Perhaps you'd like to talk over Skype or have them respond through email. Whatever it is, make it clear.

Here's an example letter. It's short and personal and I've found it works well for opening a collaboration discussion uti-lizing email. Personalize it for your own needs if you don't al-ready have a similar template.

DEAR INFLUENCER,

We here at Acme Brand have been looking for influencers to work with long-term as part of a new initiative we're de-veloping. Everywhere we look, we find your content. Your blog posts/images/videos such as _____ and _____ really resonated with us—so much that we also shared them with our community!

We are trying to establish a deeper relationship with the types of people in your community, so we would love to find a way to work together with you. We know that you are busy and probably already work with other brands, but we are confident we can establish a relationship that is mutually beneficial and help you do more of what you love to do: Educate/entertain/inspire your community!

Would you have time for a quick phone call to explore how we could work together? Looking forward to your favor-able response.

Yours sincerely,
Neal Schaffer
Director of Influencer Relations

The introduction is formal. You're making a business connection here. A conversational tone probably isn't appropriate (although it might be depending on the branding and demographic of the influencer or your brand). You draw attention to their content and point out what resonated with your brand and why. You play to what they want to bring to their community, showing that you have an understanding of their goals. The letter shows that you both want same things and asks the question: How can we work together? The more you've engaged with them online before reaching out through email, the better received it will be. The relationship will have begun in some degree before you're asking for something.

ENGAGING THE INFLUENCER'S CREATIVITY

An often-overlooked element of influencer marketing is giving the influencer room to work their own magic on your message. As a brand, it's natural to feel possessive over your message and how you're portrayed. Letting go is an essential part of collaborating with influencers. For the influencer to be as effective as they can with your message, you have to trust them to communicate with their community.

There are many examples of a brand being too limited in how it works with the influencer. A TapInfluence study found that 40 percent of influencers felt they were not given the right creative freedoms.[9] To expand on this, a study by CrowdTap found that 50 percent of influencers felt that the creative freedom was their favorite part of working with brands.[10] It gives them a chance to play with messages, images, and all sorts of other things to a large audience. The creative freedom is essential.

In my own work as an influencer, I was approached by an agency who wanted very specific things. The campaign they were working on required the mention of a certain soon-to-be-released movie that was unrelated to the product, along with very specific lengths of Instagram stories, places where the photos were taken, and other ways the brand was mentioned. The outline read like a paid social post, not something that showed trust in my voice and a partnership. Just from looking at the brief, I could tell that these limitations would take all the fun and creativity out of working with the brand. The content would also not feel authentic and might potentially be irrelevant to my audience, hurting both my engagement as well as the brand image of the ad sponsor.

It's true that some micro-influencers might undertake a campaign like this. If they do take it on, it's likely to not lead to ongoing longer term engagement. This brief also looked to me like it was sent out en masse, trying to get a broad engagement without investing the proper time to develop relationships. This is what I strongly believe you want to avoid. This style of brief approaches influencer marketing like a short-term paid media post. It's not a relationship and not a partnership. It overlooks the reason you want to engage with the influencer—their voice and their style of posts—simply to get at their audience. The result is likely a low-level short-term engagement, if at all.

Some brands like to have a statement they give influencers to paste for their posts. Some influencers like to have this arrangement, too. But if you assume this without having the conversation, particularly with an influencer who enjoys using their own voice, then you will wear out your welcome, and miss the opportunity you've worked to create. Engaging the influencer means engaging their creativity and ensuring you have a conversation about the content instead of assuming a cut-and-paste approach. Let the influencer do what they feel is best in order to get the best and most authentic engagement on behalf of your brand from their community. That's the whole point of influencer marketing, right?

Sometimes there are errors. Markelle Fultz, the number-one pick in a recent NBA draft, forgot to edit a paid post for Tissot when he posted on Instagram that he was "Excited to head to (City) and join the (team name). @Tissot.us is helping me get started with my (team name) watch."[11] Perhaps it was a simple mistake overlooked in the excitement of being drafted, but it's an error that has ramifications. It's a mistake that should be learned from. Unfortunately, the number-one NBA pick the next year, Deandre Ayton, didn't learn from it, posting his own unedited sponsored post when he was drafted.[12]

Once the terms have been agreed on and the influencer has begun posting, the work isn't over. Check out the post and see what they did with your message. You might get some ideas of how to reframe your own posts. You can share, boost, and give feedback to the post. Boosting an influencer's post about your brand will have more reach than boosting your own post with the same message. The influencer would probably like the extra exposure too. Telling the influencer that you like the post, working in some praise, goes a long way to augmenting and growing the relationship. Influencers are human, and we all like positive feedback.

Should you have the right to reuse their content, don't forget to repurpose influencer content for your organic social or even web properties. It's not surprising that more than 75 percent of marketers surveyed in a recent ACTIVATE State of Influencer Marketing Study recycle influencer content at least a couple times per quarter.

To some degree, you can think of influencers as customers, and use a similar approach to your customer relationship management strategy. Look at ways to bring them into your marketing initiatives. Perhaps they have ideas too. This is where the relationship moves toward a much longer collaboration. You trust them and they trust you. Interest in both sides helps you both achieve your goals. The continued relationship management will bring dividends over time.

THE TOOLS OF THE
INFLUENCER MARKETING TRADE

S ocial media is in a state of constant change. Everything moves so quickly that even talking about social media tools is a challenge. In my books, articles, and presentations, I've always attempted to discuss concepts regarding tools rather than specific technical details. Technology and the details, along with the companies that offer the tools, will always change. I can name as many tools and companies that have over disappeared the last decade as those who have survived. The fundamental concepts behind the tools, however, do not change.

The aim here is to focus on the concepts of the tools since the functionality can be inefficient or confusing. The tools listed below cover the main groups of influencer marketing tools: tools for analysis, marketplace tools, agencies, and search engines. The amount of data and tools themselves can be overwhelming. These tools and this guide can help navigate them and provide you with a starting point.

THE ROLE OF TOOLS

The process of influencer identification can be very data intensive. There's so much data to gather, and just as many ways to interpret the data, that it's nearly impossible to do manually in any thorough way. That's where tools help. Marketers love tools. They are part of the scaling approach of any business program:

People => Process => Tools

I'm such an evangelist of social media-related tools that I co-founded a now defunct event called the Social Tools Summit to discuss the ways technology can help all facets of social media marketing. The summit addressed the best practices in applying the technology to social media marketing-related topics. I'm an even stronger believer that tools don't, and can't, replace processes. You start with a strong process, then find the tool to help you become more efficient and accurate at implementing that process.

The influencer marketing industry has matured to the point where there is a tool available for almost any challenge with influencers that you might have. While most recent marketer surveys indicate that measuring the ROI of influencer marketing is the most challenging subject today, identifying the right influencers to work with is usually not far behind in the results. In fact, Mediakix's recent Influencer Marketing Industry Benchmarks report indicated that 61 percent of marketers agree that it is still challenging to find the best influencers for a campaign. Beyond the question of ROI and finding or identifying influencers, tools also cover elements of pitching to and maintaining communications with influencers, paying influencers, and tracking performance on key indicators.

If a tool or platform is performing all of the above functions, including compensating influencers on your behalf, then the logical assumption is that influencers opted into this service. All of the tools have a different database of influencers. They collate their pools differently. Some tools act as marketplaces and are opt-in only. This is convenient, but it is also an indication that you're only accessing a limited subset of influencers compared to what is out there, and what will show up with other search engines. Some tools don't let you pay or manage influencer relations through their dashboard, but they allow you to communicate or track spending or ROI. This is where you decide what is convenient and what you will do in a more manual approach.

Marketplaces are another field of tools that help manage influencer identification and relationships. Many of these are opt-in for the influencer, meaning that, once again, you're exposed only to a subset of influencers. That being said, many brands and agencies do appreciate the convenience that these marketplaces have to quickly and easily source and launch a campaign with influencers.

JCLUB

AS A STARTUP, GAINING ATTENTION FOR YOUR brand in the sea of internet companies is a huge hurdle. Standing out and building a reputation when you're fresh and new is not easy. Is it possible to build a strong reputation quickly? How can working with influencers bring visibility to your brand?

When jClub, an online shopping portal, looked at spreading the word about their new store, they turned to influencer marketing. The goal was to engage with around thirty bloggers to increase brand awareness and drive sales. By engaging with bloggers in this way the brand would also generate a wealth of online material that would point customers to the store in the future. In this case, ¡Club was quite set in the way they wanted the bloggers to describe and promote the brand.

With the help of the marketplace tool dealspotr, ¡Club worked with thirty-three influencers who produced a total of ninety-nine pieces of content including thirty-one dedicated blog posts, twenty-six Facebook posts, thirty-one Tweets, and two YouTube videos.[1] The influencers were given affiliate codes to pass onto their audience, further incentivizing the bloggers' engagement.

The return was impressive. For a total spend of $2,923 over 33 influencers, and an investment of 7.5 hours in campaign management, ¡Club took in $16,255 over 378 sales. That's a staggering 550 percent return on marketing spend.

A search engine is the final category of tool, and it is truly open. A search engine requires more involvement from your end, including more filtering and searching by hand. Again, you have to understand what each search engine offers. There are different scopes for talent agencies, marketing agencies, and marketplaces. Some agencies or search engines flag accounts as influencers when they have 10,000 followers, but there might be a micro-influencer with 5,000 followers who is more influential and better targeted for your brand's needs. Every database has a different scope, and you have to understand what you're dealing with and raise questions to understand what you're looking for.

Some agencies or marketplaces have filters, but it's when you get to the search engines and the broader tools without the opt-in methods that you get the most filters. These tools all have different filters and serve different functions. Understanding the possibilities and seeing what's feasible are the first steps.

Here's a sample of some of the filters that most influencer search engines provide:

Audience size—an obvious filter and possibly the first one people look at when considering influencers

Engagement rate—a more important metric to see how much of the audience is actually listening and engaged

Reach—expanding on audience and showing how many potential impressions the influencer gets, rather than just audience size

Amplification—measuring how often the influencer's content is shared and amplified through the networks

Social network—which networks the influencer operates across

Relevance—measured with different filters for different tools regarding topic or other things we know about the influencer

Beyond these common filters, I find the further metrics below to be essential in the refining process of identification.

Audience demographics—Just who is their audience made up of? The usual demographic statistical categories of countries, cities, languages, ages, authenticity, education, income level, etc. are all worth sorting through. The level and detail of information can be scary when you see how much data can be filtered. Further details such as interests, hashtags, categories, and mentions are valuable filters.

Lookalikes—A powerful device to find and match influencers. There are tools that find the influencers you're looking at and then say: If you're interested in these influencers then perhaps you'll be interested in these, too, since the audiences are similar. Engaging with lookalike influencers can be a powerful step to expand your program and might expose you to relevant influencers you would not have discovered on your own.

Hypr (https://hyprbrands.com/) is one influencer search engine that takes information about a social media account and creates an anonymous profile, linking similar accounts. The tool tracks social interactions of the more than one billion accounts in their database, monitoring over 100 billion interactions each month. The data identifies accounts that inspire a large amount of interaction and reactions, measuring the relevant context as well. The example Hypr gives is that Justin Bieber is able to inspire a large amount of reaction, much more than Gary Kasparov, but not in the context of chess. Obviously, Kasparov inspires more in that context and so is more relevant for that audience or topic.

Tools for reporting and keeping track of the return on investment cover content tracking and KPI reporting; spend per like, per comment, or per view; the measurement on redirect or short links; hashtag tracking by date; along with many other metrics. There are different ways the tools gather data for you, just as there are different ways to measure if the campaign was a success.

This is an overview to the landscape to give you an idea where to start in searching for tools that can help you find, engage with, and manage relationships with influencers. It's not a comprehensive list. There are many changes over time as names change, and startups fizzle out or change focus. An updated list of changing names and tools can be found at https://nealschaffer.com/influencer-marketing-tools.

It should be noted that I have done my best with the various clarification of tools, but in reality there are many overlaps. Just as Hootsuite started out as an agency and developed their own social media dashboard, which became their main business after providing their technology to other companies, some influencer marketing agencies have developed their own tools that they now provide to non-agency clients. Similarly, some influencer discovery tools or marketplaces also offer agency services. I have tried to focus on what I believe is the main benefit that each company brings to the table, but keep in mind that these overlaps exist in almost every category.

SOCIAL LISTENING TOOLS

These types of tools are designed to know who is talking about you or your competitors and can cover subjects, hashtags, and drill down to who is actually posting. They're about monitoring brand reputation. The ten listed here are industry leaders backed with a solid reputation, all with different specializations.

Awario	awario.com
Brand24	brand24.com
Brandwatch	brandwatch.com
Digimind	digimind.com

Keyhole	keyhole.co
Meltwater	meltwater.com
Mention	mention.com
Netbase	netbase.com
Sprinklr	sprinklr.com
Talkwalker	talkwalker.com

BLOGGER OUTREACH TOOLS

Before social media matured, blogging was the original source of online influence. The power of bloggers is still strong. If you're focused on bloggers, regardless of social media, this subset requires its own dedicated tools. These tools are a superior focus on blogger outreach.

BuzzStream	buzzstream.com
GroupHigh	grouphigh.com
Ninja Outreach	ninjaoutreach.com
Ontolo	ontolo.com
PitchBox	pitchbox.com

TRADITIONAL INFLUENCER DISCOVERY TOOLS

After blogging, the evolution of social media influence moved toward social networks. These three tools have been around since before social media became predominantly visual. They are backed by a long history with respect to social media and experience. They boast rich functionality and are extremely well-educated in the space. Each of the tools are a bit different and work off different algorithms because of where they started.

They are perhaps better known for B2B engagement but are certainly not limited to that field.

Klear	klear.com
Onalytica	onalytica.com
Traackr	traackr.com

INFLUENCER DISCOVERY TOOLS

These tools recognize that a large portion of social media budgets are going to visual media and focus on that, but each with their own angle. For that reason, they are primarily Instagram-centric platforms but have functionality beneficial outside of that one platform. They differ from the influencer marketplace list to follow in that they are not based on individual influencers opting in to their platform. These tools, instead, focus on developing technology to allow you to easily filter through millions of user profiles to find the perfect influencer.

AspireIQ	aspireiq.com
Grapevine	grapevinelogic.com
Grin	grin.co
Hypr	hyprbrands.com
Mavrck	mavrck.co
Neoreach	neoreach.com
Open Influence	openinfluence.com
Scrunch	scrunch.com
Trendkite	trendkite.com
Upfluence	upfluence.com

INFLUENCER MARKETPLACES

As mentioned before, influencer marketplaces often involve a subset of influencers who have opted into these platforms. The pool you identify and draw from might be smaller, but the marketplace gives you convenience as well as potential vetting by the marketplace before allowing them to be registered. These marketplaces help you source, pitch, and often handle payment through the platform. Again, they all have their different focuses with different possibilities for connecting with influencers. Shoutcart focuses entirely on Instagram shout outs. ExpertVoice is another interesting platform. The influencers listed are experts in a niche. They've often worked heavily in a type of retail and have the expertise to suggest which skiing equipment, camping gear, or painting supplies people should use for their situation. These influencers are often backed with blogs. Famebit started as a YouTube-based platform and is now currently owned by Google.

ExpertVoice	expertvoice.com
Famebit	famebit.com
Influence.co	influence.co
Intellifluence	intellifluence.com
IZEA	izea.com
Linqia	linqia.com
Shoutcart	shoutcart.com
SocialPubli	socialpubli.com
TapInfluence	tapinfluence.com
Tomoson	tomoson.com

HEALTH-ADE

AS COMPANIES LOOK MORE TO INFLUENCERS for engagement, and influencers increasingly make themselves available, how can a brand know what to look for in an influencer? How can a brand recognize what the influencer can bring to the table and if their followers are the real deal instead of bots artificially boosting the numbers?

Once you identify which influencers you want to work with there remain the time-consuming issues of working on terms of payment and terms of engagement. Engaging and managing relationships with influencers, particularly when the communication is almost always all online, can be difficult.

Increasingly, there are tools to solve this problem. These tools—both apps and companies—work as a platform and go-between to handle the mundane details for the brand when working with influencers. Health-Ade Kombucha faced these issues when looking at engaging influencers with their product. Rather than approaching each influencer individually, Health Ade utilized the tool Trend to engage with influencers.

Trend (https://trend.io) is a marketplace that lays the groundwork for brands and influencers to work together. Before listing the influencer, Trend ensures the influencers' credentials and followers are legit. Brands can post expectations of the interactions with customized requirements along with new products. When a brand and influencers take a liking to each other, they can communicate directly through the app. It's Tinder for brands and influencers.

In the case of Health-Ade, they decided how they wanted to interact with brands and used Trend to connect with influencers across the United States, without having to worry about the filtering process. The influencers received their sample product and engaged with Health-Ade Kombucha in their own way—some cooked with the product, others turned it into a cocktail or showed how they blended it into their workout regime. The results were over 135 high-quality images taken from the unique perspective of the influencer, resulting in 15,000 engagements on Instagram. The campaign pushed Health-Ade Kombucha's popularity and visibility to become one of the nation's leading kombucha brands.

By using Trend, the brand retains control over the influencer posts by approving what is posted. They are also able to still pinpoint the influencers who they feel best represent the brand ethos, image, and target demographic. The brands are also able to download the collected content influencers create to be able to use in further marketing material. These extra benefits of the interactions with influencers make the whole engagement fluid.

INFLUENCER MARKETING AGENCIES

While an agency is not a tool per se, it can provide tremendous assistance at every step of your influencer marketing activities. Some of the above-mentioned tools also have consulting or agency branches that can assist you. The ten listed below are agency leaders I've found through my own work and research. Many of these do produce a lot of content themselves, including blog posts and so on that give insights into the influencer marketing landscape to prove their expertise in the space.

360i	360i.com
Acorn	acorninfluence.com
Clever	realclever.com
Collectively	collectivelyinc.com

Influence Central	influence-central.com
Mediakix	mediakix.com
The Cirqle	thecirqle.com
Obviously	obvious.ly
VaynerMedia	vaynermedia.com
Viral Nation	viralnation.com

OTHER TOOLS

These other tools don't fit neatly into a category but are useful. Collectively, they look at details across the board, from analyzing fake influence to finding influence in content creation to helping you curate user-generated content from influencers.

BuzzSumo	buzzsumo.com
Curalate	curalate.com
FollowerWonk	followerwonk.com
HypeAuditor	hypeauditor.com
Launchmetrics	launchmetrics.com
Nimble	nimble.com
Perlu	perlu.com
Pixlee	pixlee.com
Right Relevance	rightrelevance.com
Socialix	socialix.com

In addition to my own recommendations, if you are looking for a simple list of enterprise-grade influencer marketing tools to begin researching, Forrester has published their own report on the leading influencer marketing solutions, which from their perspective comprise Ahalogy, AspireIQ, Collective Bias, Influential, IZEA, Klear, Launchmetrics, Linqia, Mavrck, Octoly, and Traackr.[2]

Using these tools is about understanding technology and processes. I cannot stress enough how important it is to not start initially with the tools. Tools are designed to help do what you're already doing, and to maximize the processes that you're already undertaking. Tools are there to assist. If you start your program with tools, then you'll get lost. You'll be presented with data points that you haven't decided how to use or how to manipulate and understand to refine your processes. When you start with process and human analysis, then you know which data you need to refine your processes. You'll understand which tools to engage. The tools are powerful and present a lot of data. It's up to you to understand which data you need and how to act on it. If you're overwhelmed with data or design your influencer program without considering what you want to achieve first, then you'll be lost. Tools are there to *support* the work you do, not *be* the work you do.

14

MEASURING YOUR INFLUENCER MARKETING ROI

After initially working through strategy and identification and then putting your program into place, there comes the time to take stock. Measuring the return is essential and, to some degree, the most important part of the process. Without proving the benefits and returns on spend, the worth of influencer marketing budget and other decisions concerning proceeding with the influencer program can't be finalized. It's a harder argument to make. From another angle, without measuring the success of what you have already done, you're unable to tighten the process. When you take into consideration what returns you have, and how your KPIs have been addressed, then you can settle into the Deming Cycle of adjusting what you're doing to refine the processes and maximize your investment.

Make no mistake, even if you're not paying influencers, it's an investment in gifting product and/or time. Properly measuring the return of this investment is essential. But just how do you measure something as fluid as influencer marketing? As

early as at least 2010, companies were looking at how to measure the return on social media. It might not be rocket science,
but it does take effort to make a strategy. McKinsey & Company began talking about "word-of-mouth equity" as a way to
measure the sales impact of a brand message that has been mul-
tiplied by word-of-mouth messaging.[1] When extended and ex-
trapolated, this clearly covers influencer marketing. This gauge
of word-of-mouth equity is not how you will measure your
influencer return, but it does provide a basis for understanding
how to measure something that seems unmeasurable.

Essentially "word-of-mouth equity" breaks down into several
points to consider.

Volume x Impact = Word-of-Mouth Equity

Volume of message—Simply stated, the more messages
you put out, the more return you get.

Impact of message—This point is broken into several factors. The first is the network—where is the influencer talking, on a scale of being an open network or not? More
important is whether or not the speaker is trusted. The
second: Who is talking and what influence do they hold?
Third, what is the message content and relevance to your
brand? And the final factor is the trigger. If the influencer
is talking about their experience with the product, the personal investment in recounting their experience is more
powerful than something based on hearsay.

When these factors are weighted and pulled into a formula
like the one above, we begin to understand how to measure the
weight of social media messages. A small number of messages
on point from someone who is trusted and influential can de-

liver a far higher return than a year's worth of disconnected messages to a larger audience.

The same 2010 *McKinsey Quarterly* article explained that in Germany, Apple's iPhone had a share of 10 percent of word-of-mouth volume. The leading smartphone brand boasted a share of 15 percent. Apple was able to leverage messages about the iPhone launching in other countries ahead of its German launch, leading to 30 percent more word-of-mouth equity than the leader. Of this share, three times more influential voices were recommending the iPhone. When these factors were considered, it became clear sales attributed to this word of mouth and social media messaging outstripped the traditional advertising six times over.

There will be ROI on your influencer marketing investment, it's just a question of how much and how you measure it. After working with influencers to spread your message, you will get more impressions, more views, and more followers. Some of these data points might not be important to you. In that case, there's no reason to measure that point. Initially, you have to decide what is important to you and how you plan to measure it, then consider how much it will cost.

There are a few studies regarding the ROI of influencer marketing that are often quoted in influencer marketing circles that give some indication that influencer marketing ROI has been proven for some time.

Burst Media published a study based on forty-eight influencer marketing programs showing that for every dollar spent on influencer marketing, you'll earn an average $6.85 back.[2] The results varied greatly depending on industry. Food and apparel earned more than $10 per dollar spent, but home and garden earned less than a $1 return. When you consider how much it costs to simply advertise on paid media, your requirements and goals, and what you want to achieve with influencer marketing, then you will have a different gauge and the ROI will vary.

A similar study by Tomoson showed that, when they surveyed over 150 influencers, the average return was $6.50, with 70 percent earning at least $2 on a dollar spent.[3] The top 13 percent earned over $20 for each dollar spent. That sort of return is impressive in any kind of scale.

A more recent study shows slightly lower yet still solid ROI for influencer marketing. In the Influencer Marketing Hub Influencer Marketing Benchmark Report for 2019, NeoReach examined more than 2,000 influencer campaigns and calculated that earned media value averaged 5.2 times per $1 spent.

WHAT DO YOU MEASURE?

Earlier in this book, I discussed the importance of deciding what exactly you wanted to achieve with your influencer marketing program. I stressed that understanding what your goals are and how they relate to your key performance indicators is essential to understanding how to measure influencer marketing success. Each KPI has its own element to measure.

Increase brand awareness	Share of voice, impressions and views
Amplify reach	Impressions and views
Grow engagement	Clicks, comments, shares; impressions and views
Grow community	Follower growth
Expand email database	New subscribers
Increase website traffic	Referred traffic
Expand product awareness	Mentions, reviews, etc.
Generate leads or sales	UTM tracking
SEO	Back links and ranking
Ad spend ROI	Cost per mention, per click, etc.

Understanding and knowing what your exact goal is and defining what metric to best measure that is key to measuring the success of your influencer program. It also gives you insights into how to refine the next round of influencer engagement to trim the fat and push your goals further.

Essentially, revenue is the most important metric. Although clicks and shares were favored by some marketers who responded in the Tomoson study, and sometimes influencer programs are started with a key goal being increased brand awareness, 56 percent of marketers said that revenue is the king indicator. If there's an increase in sales and income, then it's hard to argue that the program isn't working. This is the point where the other KPIs will help you refine your processes. Mediakix's "Influencer Marketing 2019 Industry Benchmarks" showed that increasing brand awareness and reaching new audiences were more frequent overarching goals of a brand's influencer marketing strategy than generating sales. In all of these categories and metrics, it's a measure of brand awareness and engagement.

If you prefer to measure brand awareness metrics such as impressions, likes, comments, views, and shares, you should already have the specific values of these formulated from your paid social campaign data or from your internally developed earned media valuation. Sideqik's Defining Success in Influencer Marketing will provide you some industry guidelines for these values if you don't have your own internal guidelines.

MEASURING YOUR SUCCESS

After deciding what your measuring stick will be, you must source data. A good number of the tools mentioned in chapter 13 cover many of the data points or source the data for you.

Beyond these, it's possible to measure from your internal website analytics program such as Google Analytics as well as the data provided by each social network. These can all provide a great deal of information to identify the return. There is also public social data and some that we can access without difficulty. Reported data from analytics tools or from issuing a unique URL to each influencer in order to measure click-through is also an invaluable source of data.

Instagram and its parent company Facebook are taking this one step further by allowing brands direct analysis to metrics coming from sponsored posts published by authorized influencers as well as giving brands the ability to boost influencer content to the brand's fans. This provides the additional convenience of collecting data that would otherwise be tedious to collate, difficult to access, or cumbersome to collate into one dashboard. It also makes the data transparent, trustworthy, and accurate.

Tools and platforms often collect this information, but it's collated in ways that are manipulated or sorted differently, giving you a different perspective and various analyses depending on your needs. This is what makes these tools and platforms disparate in the first place.

Using tools like this will show you a lot of data accurately and quickly. There are limitations if you're measuring ROI by different standards, but tools show you what you need to know, depending on your focus.

WHAT IS THE RETURN?

The return on your investment comes down to three simple questions:

What was your objective?
Did you achieve it?
At what cost?

With those three questions answered, you'll have a solid view of where you stand. At this point it's also worth looking at how the influencer program performed compared to other marketing channels. Did it outperform the traditional sales approach, like the German iPhone example? Did it complement other channels? Were there other benefits, such as bringing new followers and increasing brand awareness or positive sentiment? These are all benefits that engaging with influencer marketing can bring your brand, but knowing which one is key to your campaign is essential to deciding where to focus. We take a macro perspective to calculate ROI because there is no single tool that will cover everything. Not every tool will look at indicators for all KPIs or objectives. What helps, however, is that the tools are powerful enough to measure what you want to know.

One other important note about ROI is that it is always relative. If influencer marketing is becoming a mainstream part of the marketing mix, its KPIs should not just be measured but also compared against all other types of marketing within your organization. How did your influencer campaigns compare to your paid media? What benefits did you derive from your influencer program compared to traditional marketing initiatives? Asking these questions and probing for answers will often give you the ammunition you need to either expand your program or illuminate other areas to focus on optimizing. SocialPubli's "recent Influencer Marketing Report" surveyed 150 digital marketing professionals who said that influencer marketing ROI for them was higher than that of SEO, paid social, paid search, or email marketing.

Another intangible benefit that is often overlooked is content. In Mediakix's "recent Influencer Marketing Industry Benchmarks" survey of marketers, 82 percent said that they reuse influencer-generated content for social media or other advertising channels, with 31 percent of them saying they do so "all the time." Content creation, and the unique and personal approach influencers bring to this, is a strong draw for brands. Pixlee (https://www.pixlee.com/) is an example of a tool that focuses on getting access to content. Engaging influencers and user-generated content is the cornerstone of that particular marketplace. Many big brands are very keen on user-generated content at the moment. It brings a voice of authenticity and a different angle that a brand just can't use when talking about their own products. A brand is impersonal, no matter what strategy they use, and user-generated content gets around these impersonal hurdles. Reusing influencer content is a big incentive for brands who are looking at stepping into engaging with influencers, and it's certainly worth ensuring you have that permission to use their content in the formal agreement with influencers. Brands spend a lot of money on creating content, so this is another way working with influencers not only increases revenue but might aid in decreasing marketing expenses.

After you've measured your ROI, maximizing that return is next. Go back to the Deming Circle in chapter 10 and revisit the steps: Plan → Do → Check → Act. You can see what you might change or do differently. Perhaps you want to try another campaign type. Perhaps you want to try alternate media, engaging through stories or videos instead of solely through photos. Perhaps trying a different network will change your returns—engaging in YouTube, or moving away from Twitter if you want to engage with more visual media. Changing influencers or prioritizing certain influencers is also a great way to revise your program.

Your return on investment and campaign strengths and weaknesses are clear. It's now possible to learn from your program, maximizing future results. While this stage is about trimming the fat and making your process more efficient, influencer marketing is also always about experimenting and seeing what works. There is no hard and fast rule, and different brands with different influencers will see different results. However, with a strategy in hand and KPIs to measure, you're well on your way to being able to ascertain your return from influencer marketing spend and hopefully, utilizing the Deming Circle, always improving upon that return in kaizen, or continuous improvement, fashion.

PART FOUR

BECOMING AN INFLUENCER YOURSELF

In the past when I spoke about social media, most of the questions I received were about social media strategy and ROI—or about social media tools that I recommend. Increasingly, those questions have become about influencer marketing and recently, after speaking to a group of MBA students at USC, the question had evolved to: "How do I become an influencer?"

Becoming an influencer has grown to be the new trend for the younger generation who want to monetize their voices and social media platform skills. The visibility of influencers working with recognizable brands, along with the ability to engage with them and the glow of monetary success, has promoted the feeling that "if they can do it, so can I." The concept of becoming an influencer, however, is not just for teenagers who want to showcase their fashion sense, to have their voices heard, or find other ways of working with brands. In this new digital media of democratized information creation and publication, there are many advantages for businesses to yielding influence.

What if your business was the most influential voice in your industry? What if when businesses looked to work with influencers, they wanted to work with you? This brings benefits from both sides of the social media and influence coin, both measurable and intangible.

15

WHY AND HOW EVERY BUSINESS SHOULD BECOME MORE INFLUENTIAL

The rise of social media has led to the democratization of information for both distribution and consumption. This extends to the democratization of influence in the media. The importance of this shift to reach demographics is most strongly seen in demographics that increasingly lose trust in the traditional forms of media. In fact, trust in mass media in the United States has recently been at an all-time low.[1]

With all of this considered, any brand that ignores this shift or doesn't adapt to it risks redundancy. This wouldn't be the first time that resisting shifting media has been the downfall of companies.

For decades, Sears was a leading retailer with a mail-order catalog that was second to none. The catalog was a pioneering force in a shift to mail ordering, but a myriad of forces including the company's difficulties adapting to the internet age meant that Amazon became what Sears could have been. Sears lost their stronghold on the market and their role as a credible influence—and officially filed for bankruptcy.[2]

It's dangerous to ignore new avenues and to rely only on the traditional means for spreading your brand message. Not only do you miss large parts of your audience, you risk losing more with each change in social networking. As time goes on, this means generations of consumers. As with many things online, the cycle gets quicker and quicker with each developing and emerging social network and differing demographic. Consumers will find other ways to get information and you'll lose media influence quickly.

More than two-thirds of Americans get news from social media.[3] These sources have replaced newspapers and television news. Social media is so influential that, as we've seen with recent events, the rise of fake news and social media bubbles has influenced how people vote. This is why it's important, in general, for businesses to yield more influence on social media. Building influence in your own brand's loyal communities and demographics, within your own niche and area of expertise, is essential.

SOCIAL MEDIA PARTICIPATION

Several years ago, I spoke at the iStrategy conference in London where I had the chance to see Bruce Daisley, UK Sales Director for Twitter, speak. During his presentation he revealed that 60 percent of Twitter users don't tweet. It's not a statistic that Twitter is worried about since these users are still involved in consuming the content. In fact, most users on social media don't create content. Most people on YouTube don't produce videos. Most people on Instagram don't post photographs.

For well over a decade the rule of thumb concerning social media engagement across platforms has generally run along the

90–9–1 ratio (see Figure 15.1).[4] Simply put, 90 percent of the users on a network only consume content. A further 9 percent occasionally engage with the content, making up the community. The content itself is only made by 1 percent. The model can also be inverted to say that 1 percent of users create 90 percent of content, and so on. The phenomenon, attributed to Jakob Nielsen, was noted in the early days of weblog use (before anyone called them *blogs*). The same figures were found in the formative days of YouTube, and in the emergence of Yahoo! Groups.

Since only 1 percent of users create 90 percent of the content, there is a small percentage of people creating the content that everyone else consumes. Considering this, it's easy to see how influencers use content to influence. This is especially true for influential consumer recommendations. A McKinsey study

THE 90–9–1 RULE

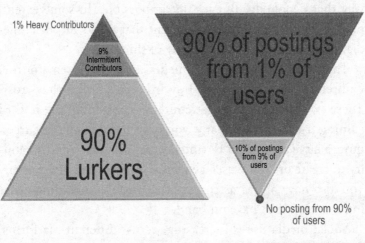

SOURCE: JAKOB NIELSEN / NIELSEN NORMAN GROUP

Figure 15.1

found that active influencers accounted for a disproportionate share of total online recommendations, with certain categories such as clothing and shoes having an influential 5 percent of users accounting for 45 percent of the influence generated.[5]

Influencers are the small percentage who have seen the benefit of publishing content on social media, and they've taken advantage of this way beyond mere online recommendations. Brands and companies who should be the most influential in niches aren't, simply because they're too slow. They didn't adapt or are still adapting. Creating communities for your brand, and then engaging with them in the way that influencers interact with their communities, is essential to increasing your influence. The essential difference is that you cannot think of or approach it as advertising. Even as a brand, you must approach it as a way to yield influence and to actually connect with people.

There is an inherent disadvantage in being a brand and not a person on social media. It's far more difficult for brands to create content with the same emotional resonance in the same way that people do. But it's not impossible. To some extent, brands can create emotional content that works on social media, but it requires a different way of thinking.

The essential rules of social media engagement remain true: Content is key, and people buy from those who they trust. These two truths mean that content goes a long way toward gaining trust. As a company, you have tremendous resources, quite a large amount of IP (intellectual property), and an ability to create or curate user-generated content from customers. You also have an infrastructure that people, including other influencers, don't have on hand.

Social media use is increasing, across different platforms, for all demographics and age groups but it still does favor millennials. In the United States, this is the biggest workforce segment, overtaking Gen-X and Baby Boomers in recent years.[6] If you're not engaged in social media, then you miss your chance to connect with this generation. Basically stated: To have any pull in media, you have to be seen on social media. This can be through celebrity representation, or working with influencers, but you will still need to be involved in social media yourself to some extent.

THE POTENTIAL BUSINESS BENEFITS OF YIELDING SOCIAL MEDIA INFLUENCE

Engaging in community building and development brings an array of benefits. There are two approaches to creating influence as a business—branded, and brand agnostic. Not long before Instagram became huge, I was working with a client focused on the baby and new mothers sector. They were mostly looking to work with mommy bloggers. Our research uncovered a website called BabyCenter. It was a pure pay-to-play deal and the client was happy to be involved with them. The client saw Baby-Center as a key to influencing their customers and target demographic across all digital media. However, when you look closer you find that BabyCenter is actually Johnson & Johnson. They created BabyCenter as an information resource and a community for a particular subset of their customer base: young families and expectant couples. This is a perfect example of building a brand agnostic channel. Johnson & Johnson separated Baby-Center from their brand and developed it as a new media channel with strong influence in a particular niche. The brand itself might be too broad, or have a different image, to have the personal credibility that they were seeking. By establishing a separate name through the brand agnostic approach, they were able to tap into the niche they were targeting and become the most influential player in the sector. While there are many Instagrammers competing with BabyCenter for mindshare, they have successfully translated their digital influence to the social network where they currently have hundreds of thousands of fans and could thus be considered a middle influencer to engage with.

Every year I have spoken at the social media marketing industry's largest annual conference, Social Media Marketing World in San Diego. I was approached one year by a man who had read my previous book. From the way he spoke, I assumed that he was using social media strategy for B2B marketing. His strategy was something different. He was a B2B marketer using social media strategy to influence B2C companies by leveraging consumers. His company was a large-scale flower wholesaler and his primary market was supermarkets. Across the United States, and in the particular states where he operated, there are only a handful of supermarket chains. His aim was to influence the buyers at these chains. Augmenting the orthodox approach of directly engaging with these leading supermarket chains, he built social media communities of passionate flower lovers. After these communities were developed and thriving, he then went back to the supermarket chains and showed them the budding communities of flower lovers. He said that if the supermarkets worked with them, then his company could influence these communities to go to their stores. This similarly brand agnostic approach is how his company differentiated themselves from other flower brands. First and foremost, the online communities were flower lovers, but he was able to harness the strength in their numbers to leverage his brand.

The same concept underscores the approach with a branded channel. The more influence you yield, then the more powerful your position is when you approach a company like a Costco or a Walmart and show the thriving and passionate community you have behind you. This community is yours to leverage retailers to sell their products. I addressed a group of U.S. State legislators with a similar message, telling them exactly that: You want to yield more influence. Donald Trump is the first influencer who became president. When he tweets, people listen, and this is something that happened long before he was sworn in as president. Perhaps now more people listen because of the office he holds, but his Twitter feed was an influential tool before that. This is what I think every business should aim to become: When you publish on social media, people listen.

The interesting thing here is that the more influential you become as a brand, the more it will help you with your influencer strategy. Influencers love to work with influential brands. It makes them look better, and it goes nicely on their resume. Influencers are proud of their status and name drop that they've worked with a brand that everyone has heard of, a brand that yields influence. If you bring the influencer prestige through working with you, then they might even offer more preferential terms than if you were unknown. It's also true that the more influence you yield, the more likely that the influencers or their communities have some established affinity for you, making the next steps easier. It also increases the chance that they respond to your outreach, compared to a brand that is relatively unknown.

Seeing is believing. Being seen keeps your message in front of people. Being seen brings social proof about the brand compared to those who have less influence or no social influence or social proof. It was Dr. Robert Cialdini who proposed this theory of social proof, that we rely on behaviors and opinions of others to inform our own.[7] Just as the size of the crowd in a restaurant may influence us to choose that restaurant over an empty restaurant next door, or the way that adding a laugh track to a television show will encourage us to laugh along, social media works as validation. It works as social proof of our own choices, in the way that testimonials validate a choice.

Being influential also helps your inbound influencer marketing. Beyond being more receptive to your outreach, the more influential your brand is, the more influencers will reach out to you to work together. Naturally, having more influencers who are working with you will draw even more influencers who want to work with you.

BUILD TO YIELD

Becoming influential is conceptually simple. Figure 15.2 shows the four steps of building influence. As with most things in life, it's the execution that's a little more challenging.

THE FOUR STEPS OF BUILDING INFLUENCE

Figure 15.2

The first step is in defining your brand for content. This should be an extension of your existing strategy. What is your brand? What content can you produce? You have to publish content that is high-quality and authoritative. It must be unique to your brand and company. Defining a visual language, as covered in previous chapters, goes along with this. The next step is publishing regularly. Whether it's uploading videos, publishing articles, or tweeting frequently, the content must be published consistently.

This is the point where many brands stop. They have their content strategy, they have their platform and publishing, but building social media influence is more than just publishing content. They publish content that might be of high quality with regularity and hope for it to build a community, instead of engaging with the community. Interacting with what other people post, not always about your brand but within your niche and your community, is where you go beyond being a strong brand and become an influential voice. Engage with followers, ask questions of them. Social media allows conversations, and many brands don't converse. They use their social media strictly as a platform to broadcast messages. Building trust comes from engaging with followers and users, fans and customers, on a personal level. Nurturing relationships takes time. Staying engaged also brings other results, letting you stay on top of trends. In some cases, you'll become a trend-setter yourself.

This is an organic way to send social signals that you're interested in the community. You will build followers around you. On each platform there are different ways of doing this. On Twitter you can follow, favorite, retweet, mention, direct message, add to a list . . . all different ways to send signals that you like what they're saying and you're into the conversation. As mentioned earlier, when looking to engage with influencers, use social signals.

CLIMB THE INFLUENCER LADDER

There used to be a tool called Klout that measured the scale of someone's influence—the level of their audience engagement, and how far that reached. It was an extremely useful tool that provided an easy to understand Social Score from 0 to 100 based on one's influence. Unfortunately it's not around any longer. An alternative that I like to recommend is RightRelevance (https://rightrelevance.com), a tool I talked about in a previous chapter. RightRelevance adds some extra features too. Using this tool, it's easy to check who is influential in your field and add them to your list. You can engage with them and nurture the relationship.

If you've already gone through the influencer identification phase of your influencer marketing strategy, you already know the influencers you want to add to your network. Using a third-party social scoring tool like RightRelevance allows you to leverage their data analysis based on social signals as to who has influence based on what keyword, a convenience that allows you to quickly build a database as well as a specific measure of influence so that you can chart how well your company's efforts perform as a KPI. While no social scoring mechanism is 100 percent accurate, it's a convenient tool to utilize the measurement of your brand compared with others.

Plotting out a database of your community charts the territory you're entering and will show you something of a path through to influence. Understanding who are the most vocal influencers in the terrain is essential work to gaining a foothold for yourself. When you chart the 9 percent who will join the discussions and the 1 percent who are the content creators and the largest voices in the field, the strategy is cut out for you.

This database, or list of users or however you decide to set it up, shows you the rungs of influence. It charts a course so you know how to climb it. Using a tool for management, or even just using a spreadsheet, will help you keep track of who is who, who is influential, and who is gaining influence. Some platforms have a way to manage these groups of people, like adding people to lists in Twitter.

Once the territory is mapped, you can see who is sharing the content and whose content is worth sharing from the point of view of building influence. Comment and engage with those who have a bigger influence than you. This might not be those with bigger numbers of followers, of course, but a stronger following in the niche in which you're operating.

Share germane content from these relevant influencers and voices, and even curate content and use your influence to share content by others. When others share your content, add them to a list so you remember they like what you're posting. Send them a comment or some sign that you noticed the engagement. It goes both ways—share and share alike. However, if you share content and notice that those whose content you're sharing aren't sharing yours or even acknowledging it, then cut them from the list and move on. Take a look at the list each month and work through the score to revise whose content you will share and with which voices you'll comment and engage.

As you build more influence yourself and engage in more conversations with influencers, you will slowly become a source of information for the community and find an increase in your community members. The larger your following grows and the more influencers who mention you, the more influence you will be perceived to have. You will be on your way to growing your influence in the specific communities you choose to engage in.

To recap, building a community, forging trust, and creating influence comes through engagement over time. You will gain more followers and you'll have others sharing your content.

With time, your engagement means that you'll be perceived as being part of the discussion, and so you'll be seen as having influence. Remember to use your employees and existing brand advocates to help spread your message and to share their content too. Those with existing affinity for your brand are a powerful resource to bring you a following from the very beginning, and engaging with them will help accelerate your rise to influencer. This is not an exercise in marketing, so approach them with the view of being more influential.

HOW TO BECOME A SOCIAL
MEDIA INFLUENCER YOURSELF

Expanding your influence on social networks, as a brand or as an individual, brings multifaceted benefits. As a brand, if you're influential, then you'll already be involved with the discussions and conversations that influencers are engaging in, making opening doors and forging relationships somewhat easier. The gravity of your own influence will make you attractive to potential influencers looking to partner with you. As an individual, developing and growing your influence puts you in a position to be hired by a brand to help their campaigns.

So how do influencers build influence? This is the time to look at what we've been discussing throughout the book from the other side of the coin. There are different ways influencers connect with people and with brands. There are reviews, social conversations, blogs, podcasts, sharing their own photos or videos or commenting on those created by others, live streams, webinars, tweetchats, and at the other end of the spectrum, longer form work including books and public speaking. The common element here is that it all revolves around the central theme of content creation. The influencer connects with their audience through content.

Content alone is only part of the picture of building influence. If brands represent specific products or services for consumers or businesses, what will people represent? This is where the concept of personal branding, or more importantly niche, comes into play. With billions of social media users to compete with, how will your content stick out? It comes down to representing a specific niche, something you are an expert in or have a passion for that you can teach or inspire others about. When you send social signals to others who like other people representing similar niches, it will become easier for you to build a community when it is clear what specific things you post about and/or are an expert in.

It takes a large investment of time, but I believe—and I tell my agency clients this—that any company can find success in social media through generating an influential presence within three to six months.

CREATING STRATEGY

As with most parts of influencer marketing, it begins offline. Becoming more influential starts with developing a strategy. In this case, you address five key questions.

Who is your target customer? To set sail you need to have at least a general guide or map.

What is your unique passion, skill, or experience? You will need to create content about your specific niche. If you're not passionate about the topic then you'll struggle to keep going and run out of steam.

Which networks should you target? What platforms are you comfortable with?

Which content media are you most proficient in? Visual content requires a different skill-set than written content.

Which influencers should you target to collaborate with? That's right: Influencer collaboration is as helpful to brands as it can be to help you achieve influencer status faster.

The first question is possibly the most important. This is essential to what you will do and how you will build your audience. Who is your target customer? Who is going to hire you as an influencer? Who do you want to influence? Often people post on all kinds of topics, wide-ranging and across industries, in order to be heard. During webinars and while presenting on strategy, I have sometimes been asked if I do this too. Sometimes I do this on Instagram, I admit. I'll post something about Japan, something about food, and then something about soccer. But on Instagram I'm not as influential. I haven't done the work that I outline here for Instagram. I have done it for Twitter and when I tweet, I do so only on the selected topics where I've built influence.

Who will hire you as an influencer? Which brands will be attracted by your profile and the content you produce? B2B industries are still lagging behind adopting influencer marketing, with only a reported 15 percent of them engaging in influencer marketing.[1] Consumer-facing brands, however, show a very different story. In GartnerL2's Intelligence Report Influencers 2017, they analyzed more than 1,000 brands and their relationships with over 5,000 influencers and found that an average of 70 percent of brands across benchmarked consumer-facing industries were engaging in influencer marketing. More than 80 percent of brands in luxury, activewear, beauty, hospitality, and retail were already collaborating with influencers. To connect with the industry, you have to produce content that matches their message, to a degree. So, define the industry where you fit in. If you nominate multiple industries then you won't be as successful as if you pick one, simply because your approach will not be as targeted. Consider what you look for in an influencer, covered earlier in the book, and how they engage with their audience.

Once you've identified your industry, it's time to refine it and find your niche. Say your industry is fashion—it's still an extremely broad category. There's men's fashion, women's fashion, casual, outdoor fashion, swimwear, millennial fashion, urban fashion, and so on. The more specific your niche is, the easier it is for brands to find you. Look at brands you would like to work with and consider how they categorize their products. This gives you an example of the niche you'd like to work within. In a perfect world, which brand would you like to work with? Who is your ideal customer? The more you've identified them, the more accurately you can create content that will attract them.

To the second point: What is your unique expertise? It's extremely unlikely that you're the only person to blog or photograph the topic that you're addressing. There are, after all, a large number of people who want to hear about it. To stand out from the other voices in the field, you have to develop your own spin. What makes your posts uniquely your voice? There are influencers out there who, once you see the content, you know immediately who they are. The photographs have a strong visual identity, or the writing on the topic is from a personal and unique angle. What is your voice? This is a branding exercise for yourself that will flow through all the content you create. You will have to produce a lot of content and your unique voice is what will allow you to not only attract brands but equally attract followers in order to build an influential community that brands would want to tap into. People will engage with your expertise or your personality. You just have to find a way to broadcast that to them in order to build a community of people who are interested in you, and interesting to brands.

Choosing and refining your strategy to pinpoint your social network is integral. You can't be on all of them, and so you must decide where your target audience is. Trying to be on as many networks as possible can actually be detrimental to your growth. There's no point being on YouTube if you can't create enough content for it, or if you only have ten followers because you're spending more time on Twitter or Instagram where you have a lot of followers. It takes away energy and time that can be better invested. If you're on platforms where you don't have content and followers, when brands search for you, they will see that there is no activity nor engagement and this just weakens your image.

The best place to start is with the networks you're already on. Begin with what you know. If you're already aware of how to use Facebook or LinkedIn, then those are the places to start. There are a lot more networks now including Pinterest and Snapchat. Depending on your location or demographic, you might need location-specific networks like WeChat in China or LINE in Japan. Social media continues to change, and you want to make sure you're not on a platform that's dying or sinking.

The functionality for some social networks changes depending on whether you have a business account or personal profile. Business accounts are limited on Facebook and LinkedIn, and this reflects how and why we've seen influencers rise from

Instagram, Twitter, YouTube, and other networks where the personal profile and business accounts have similar functionality, such as the ability to freely follow other accounts and engage as a person would. These same social networks allow your content to be searchable, making your content more easily discoverable by potential followers or brands when looking for the relevant topic.

My general advice is to start with two networks. You don't have to be everywhere. Begin with the same content on two networks and keep track of the results. After a month you can compare how both have fared. Generally, you will see more organic engagement on Instagram, YouTube, Twitter, or Pinterest, but you can't ignore the largest networks. LinkedIn is essential for many B2B industries, and Facebook is still the biggest network for consumer-facing brands.

The platforms you use will also be decided by the medium you use to communicate. If you take lots of photos, then you'll lean toward Instagram. Videos will obviously be hosted on YouTube, but you could engage with people on Instagram, Facebook, and Pinterest as well. Visual storytelling lends itself best to Instagram or Snapchat, and with the written word you'll want a blog. If you're in the B2B sector, then you'll want to cover LinkedIn. I'd argue that in any case, you should still have a simple website to lead people to. You'll want content on your website, too, to draw people there. Studies show that companies who blog do perform better.[2] They certainly have more pages that show up in a Google search and, because of this, a more far-reaching SEO presence, meaning it's more searchable and ultimately more influential.

What about the role that those who have greater influence than you in the same or similar niche can yield? Budding influencers tapping into the greater reach of more established influencers is a common practice in the society of social media users. From taking selfies with well-known influencers at conferences to joining groups of content creators on sites such as Triberr (https://triberr.com) for more exposure on Twitter and Tailwind Tribes (https://tailwindapp.com/tribes) for greater content reach on Pinterest, social media influencers have used different platforms and methods to engage and help each other. Deciding who to target that has greater influence to a similar community you want to resonate with, therefore, becomes an important consideration.

While Triberr and Tailwind Tribes feed on the need that influencers also have for content curation to keep their social media feeds active, a more powerful way of collaborating with influencers is through guest blogging. I talked about how companies can submit and potentially get their content published on the blogs of influencers as Sponsored Content Distribution, but many influencers will look to monetize their blog popularity by charging businesses a fee for sponsored content. Individual bloggers, however, especially if they yield some influence of their own, are often welcome to blog for free.

Blog content is powerful in that it lives on forever in Google searches, can attract backlinks, and can be read and shared by the community of the influencer who publishes the blog. It goes without saying that the influencer will also be sharing your content published on their site through their RSS feed, newsletter, and social sharing. This is how you can quickly expand your reach as an influencer and accelerate the building of your community.

IMPLEMENTING THE STRATEGY

Once you've run through the self-branding exercise and identified the niche you're targeting, you're into the implementation stage. Now it's about content creation, building a following, and audience engagement. Sounds easy, right?

One way to think about content creation is in terms of buckets. Continuing the earlier example: Let's say you're posting about fashion, and women's fashion in particular. You might identify four buckets to fill and draw from for your content—casual wear, evening wear, activewear, and accessories. Working with these categories for a few weeks, you'll create content that covers each of them and post it. After several weeks of publishing the same number of posts on each of the content buckets, you'll get data identifying what your followers engage with most on which social network. You'll see trends and it will be clear what resonates most. This will give you an indication about what niche you'll develop. You might drop accessories and see that activewear does better on Instagram while casual wear does better on Facebook, so you'll refine your plan accordingly.

The algorithms on different sites will also affect the way you post. Publishing five times a day on Facebook will result in your newsfeed slowing down and hiding your posts to a degree. On Twitter, no one will mind if you post five or more times a day. In fact, on Twitter and Pinterest, you have to publish more to stand out above the noise. On LinkedIn people might wonder why you've posted five times that day. If you're publishing content on YouTube or blogging, then have a different approach simply because the content takes longer to produce. In this case it might be hard to do each day, but I would say, generally, the more the better.

At the same time, you have to build a community and make an authentic connection with them. Invite friends and follow others. After building a following for a while, you might want to add some paid social to boost a targeted following. If you have a goal of 5,000 followers in the next two months and you have 3,500 followers, adding some paid social to boost this number can help. Paid social will be targeted and not just spread over random people. Instead it will be targeted at people who have an interest in the field you're posting about, and in a targeted demographic you've identified that you want to reach in order to build your community.

Just to be clear, there is no need to buy followers. There are those who do this but boosting numbers is a façade and doesn't lead to anything that will benefit you in the long term. If you buy followers, then the content you produce will go into a smaller percentage of newsfeeds because these fake followers are not engaging. This can have a negative effect on parts of the algorithm, which will mean getting your content seen by real people becomes harder. Brands are getting better at auditing accounts and seeing how many fans are fake and how many aren't. There are more and more tools that brands can use to see what percentage of followers are real. There are cases where celebrities have lost large chunks of their followers and have been exposed as having a large percentage of fake followers. In July 2018, Twitter identified and deleted fake accounts causing celebrities like Justin Bieber, Rhianna, and even Barack Obama to lose two million followers.[3] In 2019 President Trump complained to Twitter CEO Jack Dorsey about losing 200,000 followers, to which Dorsey replied that they periodically delete fake or bot accounts.[4] When Twitter or Instagram expunge 10 million fake accounts, you could find that your followers go from 5,000 to 1,000 in a day. That's definitely not something you want, and it will affect your credibility. It's a practice that's done, but I don't recommend it. The same goes for buying fake engagement, another scheme that audit tools are getting better at measuring. Instead, follow those who have interest in what you do and those who post in the same realm. Identify those who follow other lookalike influencers and engage with their audience. Invest the time to post meaningful comments on their posts.

You should also be checking out other influencers in your niche who you think are doing a great job on your preferred social networks. Natalie Alzate, using the name Natalies Outlet, is a YouTuber with more than 10 million subscribers. She started with a few thousand subscribers, but after studying her favorite YouTubers, she tested videos in multiple genres, and beauty tips and lifehacks ended up performing well and propelling her to an influencer status over time.[5] This a classic example of applying the PDCA Deming circle to your content strategy and optimizing your content as you implement your strategy. Whether you are a brand implementing an influencer marketing strategy or a person trying to yield more social media influence, the principle is the same.

In addition, since collaborating with other influencers is a key tactic, you'll want to find ways that you can offer value to influencers in addition to all of the other social signals you should be sending them. "Offering value" means a lot of different things to different people, but they are things you can do to make the like of an influencer easier. It could be anything from mentioning them when you share their content in social media to actually writing a blog post talking about their expertise and what you learned from them. Influencers like to be acknowledged and will often share public acknowledgment to their own followers, so be creative and find ways to offer value while retaining the authenticity of your true self.

COMMUNITY BUILDING

The first step toward building a community is finding its members. Working through bio searches and looking at who other influencers are following can yield a lot of information. Who follows influencers similar to them? You can search through mentions and hashtag searches, depending on the networks you're working on. Social media gives you so much data on who to follow and how to engage with them to build your community. However, it takes time. It's steady work but if you follow and engage on a regular basis, things do happen. By constantly doing this, you'll let people know you exist, and they will begin engaging with your content.

To put it bluntly: Brands are challenged to communicate, make a connection, and build trust with people but humans do it well. This is the entire reason for influencer marketing in the first place. A great way of engaging is by taking the same steps outlined before in content curation. Regularly share content to create relationships with your fans and other influencers. You can engage with the posts of your fans, or the brands you want to work with, or influencers in a similar field. Building a following is a lot of work and it does take time to work through strategy, content, community, and engagement.

Collaborating with other influencers is a win/win situation. You can help each other with shout outs, or even just sharing content, tagging them so they know the content is being shared. Then connect with them and ask them to share your content. Helping each other out and publishing each other's content is a great way to ensure you're publishing or sharing content constantly. Sharing instead of always creating gives you more exposure too. It's not a zero-sum game. Other influencers don't have to lose for you to win, so collaborating is just more conversation. Influencing is about being part of more conversations and being listened to enough that you bring weight to what is said and you have people listening to you.

Talk about brands you want to work with and when you do mention them, tag the brands themselves. You have to bring yourself to their attention. You have to tap them on the back and show them how your audience engages with you in a way that is attractive to them. Once you feel confident that your community has been engaging with your content regarding that brand, reach out to them via DM and tell them you'd love to work with them. As the great hockey player Wayne Gretzky said, "You miss 100 percent of the shots you don't take."

You can also sign up to influencer marketplaces. This a way to be part of a searchable database—and there are a lot, as mentioned in chapter 13 on influencer marketing tools. Take a look at which ones are better aligned with what you want to do and the demographics or industry you work with.

A final and often overlooked resource is the old-fashioned email list. Email is another channel to promote campaigns. When you're working with brands on an influencer campaign, often you don't own your own content. You've agreed to give the content to the brand so they can use it again at a later date. Your intellectual property, if created for a brand as part of influencer marketing, may be their property not yours. But you own your email list. That's not something you sell or give away. Brands will also be interested in knowing what other engagement and platform you've got outside of the followers on your social network accounts. If you have an email list of several thousand, then you bring more to the table as an influencer, making you a more attractive prospect to work with for brands.

MONETIZATION

Generating an income from your influence might not be your final objective, but if it is, after following my advice with consistent publishing, collaborating, and engaging over time, you will be on your way to building a community of those who trust you and that brands will seek to tap into. You will begin to experience the flip side of this book, and while there are many brands that will heed the advice I've given and only look for relevant influencers for a long-term relationship, not every message from a brand will indicate so.

It is critical to understand that you are serving a community, and your community is your biggest asset. Every time you work with a brand, where the content was not genuinely authentically your own but influenced by an often for-profit engagement with a company, you risk alienating your influential position within your community. That's why it's important to:

Create Sponsored Posts as if They Were Your Own — The closer in authenticity your sponsored content appears next to your organic content, the better the content will perform for yourself and for the brand.

Keep a Balance Between Sponsored and Organic Content — If you become popular and every one of your posts turns out to be an advertisement, you are no longer an influencer and instead have become a media channel. While this might be attractive to some, it goes against the authenticity and ability to relate that attracted your community to you in the first place.

If You Can't Recommend the Product, Don't Advertise It — This is the easiest and quickest way to break trust with your community. Don't do it. This is why you should always ask for a free product or service if a brand wants to pay you to promote it for the purpose of testing the "recommendability" of it.

Add Value to Your Community When Working with Brands — I spoke in chapter 8 about influencer collaboration types and how giveaways and/or discounts using promo codes are often used in conjunction with gifting or other forms of collaboration. By requesting brands to do this when they collaborate with you, you are finding a way to add value to your community and deepen your trust with them.

Tag and Link to Brands Religiously—If you talk about companies that you want to work with (or get on their radar), link to and tag them whenever possible. You never know when it might generate engagement from the brand. At a minimum, it's content that you can point to when you reach out to them for the first time to show them your love for them.

At All Times Be You—You will be building community and trust around your brand. There's no need to try to pretend to be someone else or paint a different picture of who you are. It is the down-and-dirty real you that will attract those who follow you—and brands to work with you—so always be the real you.

FINAL THOUGHTS

The Future of Influencer Marketing and the Role of Artificial Intelligence

From the democratization of influence to leveraging influencers to becoming an influencer yourself, the industry of influencer marketing will continue to evolve hand-in-hand with the evolution of social media, media consumption, and technology. Now that we understand *The Age of Influence*, I would like to address a question that I often get asked after my speeches: What does the future hold for influencer marketing?

When I began working on this volume, it was my intention to write a book that would provide you sound advice many years after the publication. But the business world is being bombarded by a number of new technologies and their acronyms, such as the Internet of Things (IoT), Augmented Reality (AR), Virtual Reality (VR), Blockchain Technology, Crypto Currencies, and Artificial Intelligence (AI). I believe AI will withstand the test of time and help harness the future of influencer marketing.

At some point, influencer marketing for businesses will become part of a numbers game. It may happen quicker than expected, just as social media marketing in general did. The barrier for entry into becoming a social media user, and then developing and yielding influence, is low and has resulted in the emergence of hundreds of thousands of influencers today. This also means that, unlike traditional celebrity endorsements in which a brand may align with one or a handful of celebrities directly, new media segmentation and audience fragmentation force brands to engage with more figures who've built unique communities on different channels.

Simply because of the sheer number of potential influencers, there is a need to scale beyond human capabilities. Scaling this identification is essential to better understand many social media users' influence over a wide range of communities discussing almost anything imaginable. This is where artificial intelligence (AI) comes in. AI is already helping companies make better influencer marketing decisions.

WHY AI IS A NATURAL MATCH FOR INFLUENCER MARKETING

Recently I had a chance to work with Open Influence (OI) (https://openinfluence.com), one of the influencer discovery tool companies recommended in chapter 13, who is also one of the leaders in leveraging AI for influencer marketing. OI was looking for ways to incorporate their knowledge and experience into a scalable solution helping brands match their needs with existing social media users' communities, work, and culture. OI believed they could help brands unleash the potential for unparalleled ROI in influencer marketing. They recognized that they could achieve all this by incorporating an AI engine into their platform and programming it with unique algorithms for unsurpassed influencer identification.

What OI didn't realize immediately was how the new platform fundamentally changed the rules of influencer marketing—for good. They combined searching by keyword and not by predetermined category, visually inspecting posts including brand mentions not in text, finding "fake" influencers, and even predicting contextual performance for a specific brand, influencer, and campaign. Eventually, OI realized they had unleashed a platform forever changing influencer marketing—and potentially online advertising in general.

Scalability inherent in this objective solution cannot be valued highly enough. Without AI, image tagging would be subjective, and the friction involved in manually tagging would be prohibitive. To understand the level of work: Look at the number of influencers, multiply that by the number of content posts to tag per influencer, and then multiply that by the number of tags per content piece. Finally, consider the frequency with which you would need to dynamically update the data. It's an inhuman level of work and detail that simply cannot be done accurately by usual methods (see Figure 17.1). This is why AI was needed. Moving from a database of 5,000 to 100,000 influencers requires an obscene amount of time to properly and dynamically tag influencers and the ever-growing amount of content they publish. This was the challenge to which AI provided a compelling and scalable solution.

HOW AI REVOLUTIONIZES INFLUENCER IDENTIFICATION

Influencer identification continues to be a huge challenge for marketers. The sheer number of existing social media users and

HOW MUCH WOULD IT
TAKE TO DO A SEARCH MANUALLY?

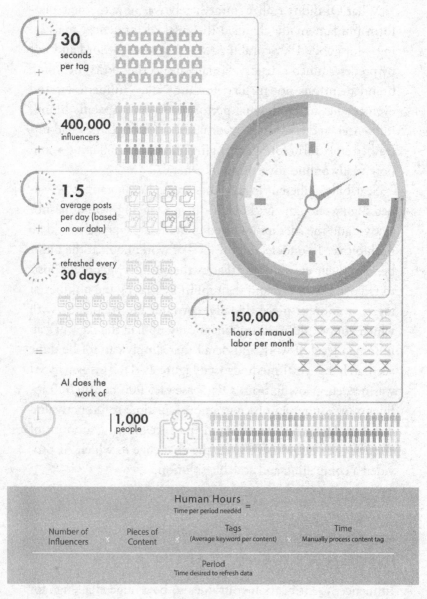

Figure 17.1

the volume of user-generated content presents an obstacle for proper identification. If you have domain expertise, possess experience in influencer marketing, and consider the different ways you could teach an AI-powered platform an objective method of identifying influencers, you will begin to realize how revolutionary AI technology is for influencer marketing today.

One of the key challenges is the industry-standard separate categorization of influencers. Brands have a need to identify the niche influencers who perfectly suit their demographic and needs, but currently the categorization is not sufficiently accurate. Influencer tagging rectifies this with searching for influencers not by broad categories but by specific tags based on actual content publishing and community-engagement history.

For instance, if an influencer was to self-categorize based on a preset list of categories, even though their "primary" type of posts were about fashion, they might also say they were into beauty, automobiles, and travel, to be considered for campaigns with a wider variety of companies. That same influencer might post a lot of fashion-related pictures. But those images might also be closely related to parenthood as they feature young children, or to sports as they showcase a new tennis outfit or swimwear at the beach. It's this kind of niche that perfectly appeals to a handful brands, and the kind of niche that communicates directly to their target demographic. Deep and proper identification in this style would save brands time and energy.

To identify the "correct" influencer, influencers need to be tagged objectively based on the contents of their own images and video rather than potentially arbitrary categories based on text or hashtags. Any companies helping brands identify influencers are responsible for this due diligence in influencer-tagging categorization. It can only be done with recent advancements in image-recognition technology, with which we can select and cross-reference millions of contextual tags identifying influencers rather than a few dozen categories (see Figure 17.2).

INFLUENCER TAGGING CATEGORIZATION USING IMAGE RECOGNITION TECHNOLOGY

Figure 17.2

BETTER UNDERSTANDING CONTEXTUAL ENGAGEMENT

Visually recognizing and dissecting an image is the gateway to uncovering unparalleled information from social media content. If an influencer posts an image with little text description and a generic hashtag like #tbt, it is simply impossible to determine the nature of the content and influence without image-recognition technology. To take this a step further visual media is often comprised of a collection of images, such as when someone is traveling in the mountains with skis mounted on a Mercedes-Benz SUV, potentially indicating three different tags.

Better understanding the contextual relationship between items in an image, their relationships with hashtags and other text being used, and different ways audiences engage with contextual relationships, helps you uncover deep insights simply not otherwise possible. Contextual engagement is another example of how image-recognition technology, once mastered, becomes an integral part of any technology platform including AI. A world of opportunities opens up for marketers to derive exponentially greater ROI from influencer marketing.

DEVELOPING ACCURATE LOOKALIKES

Facebook revolutionized social advertising in 2013 by introducing the concept of a "lookalike" audience.[1] In Facebook's words, a lookalike audience is ". . . a way to reach new people likely to be interested in your business because they're similar to your best existing customers." Within the scope of influencer marketing, these lookalikes help marketers to more quickly and accurately discover "lookalike" influencers such those influencers they have successfully worked with in the past or want to work with in the future. This can greatly reduce the time for influencer identification while helping to ensure greater success for an influencer marketing campaign.

Facebook lookalike audiences allow you to potentially find new fans and activity close to your current fanbase, visitors to your website, or even email database links. Meanwhile, AI-infused influencer marketing lookalikes allow marketers to begin with ideal influencers and model a campaign of lookalikes based on the content they post within minutes. This is another advantageous by-product of AI.

EXPOSING BOTS AND FAKE PROFILES

How AI identifies and exposes both bots and fake profiles so that marketers can steer clear is also critical. Recent fake-news scandals affecting American elections are a reminder: Every social media site is riddled with fake profiles and bots creating fake engagement and distorting numbers. Ensuring your influencer marketing program does not fall victim to these fraudulent activities is critical to your success. Fortunately, AI provides us unparalleled ways to find fake followers and expose fake engagement.

Inviting a fake profile with tens of thousands, or even potentially millions, of fake followers to be part of your influencer initiatives will add nothing to your ROI. In fact, it is estimated that fake followers in influencer marketing will cost brands more than one billion dollars a year.[2] Of course, no one purposefully invites a fake influencer to a program, but how do you know how real influencers are? AI allows us to analyze patterns indicating potential "fakeness" of a profile, for instance, analyzing the quality of the followers themselves as well as trends in follower growth to determine whether or not this influencer is real or the result of systematic fraud, or buying fake followers to potentially create a lucrative business.

Another aspect of fake profiles AI helps identify include influencers with potentially disengaged audiences (though they may be real followers). Many individuals who wish to show signs of having influence try to game the system by buying fake followers, likes, or comments. They could also participate in groups of influencers who comment or engage with each other's posts, so their content will feature more prominently in newsfeeds. A disengaged audience of an influencer might provide engagement on paper, but this engagement is gamed and has no actual business value to brands. Fortunately, AI can now identify patterns regarding the timing, nature, and source of engagement, so we can minimize the impact of disengaged audiences.

As influencer marketing grows, AI is becoming more and more critical to ensuring success for campaigns and programs.

AI can help you accurately identify the "right" influencers while also uncovering potentially negative effects on your influencer marketing ROI. Similarly, AI raises social media content's value for users. Properly leveraged AI helps you uncover unforeseen yet relevant content.

CONTENT IS THE CURRENCY OF INFLUENCER MARKETING, ENRICHED BY AI

Influencer marketing simply couldn't exist without the content created by influencers. If content is the currency of influencer marketing, being able to analyze that content is critical for identifying influencers and how influential they are in categories in which they have already been tagged. Visual-recognition technology allows us to better "tag" influencers, extending this further down into the micro level of content.

As the world of social media is increasingly visual, the text-based approach of other AI solutions is simply not effective. Text analysis is inherently limited on a visual platform such as Instagram. Furthermore, influencers don't post consecutive streams of thought in their image descriptions, often limiting thoughts to just a couple words and perhaps an emoji. Additionally, while marketers wish otherwise, hashtags aren't always used by influencers in every post, and even when they are, there is no guarantee they are aligned with the images.

This means there is a need for technical analysis with image recognition. Image recognition has typically been done manually, with an account manager looking at posts and subjectively assigning categories. Different account managers undoubtedly have different understandings of what a category like fashion or fitness entails. For example, the type of fashion depicted by Forever 21 will be completely different from Chanel. Similarly, sport drinks and gyms both engage with fitness, but in very different ways.

HOW AI HELPS GUARANTEE RESULTS

AI raises the bar by virtually guaranteeing results for influencer marketing in an unprecedented way. In addition to helping with influencer identification and content analysis, when AI is integrated into a scalable database of influencers and influencer activity, it can also help marketers better invest their influencer marketing in a number of ways.

Finding the right influencers means there is a greater chance they will participate in your program and succeed.

Vetting influencers for inappropriate content is necessary before they embarrass your brand.

Campaign modeling can be used leveraging predictive analytics and past analysis to guarantee metrics parameters such as total interactions and engagement rate prior to even beginning a campaign.

Analyzing posting frequency ensures alignment between how much we can expect an influencer to post on our behalf and the related consumption threshold of their audience for such content.

Proper AI truly helps solve issues affecting influencer marketing today, and holds great potential going forward.

ENDNOTES

Introduction

1. Jeremiah Owyang, "MySpace and Facebook Launch New Advertising Products, Why Hyper Targeting, Social Ads and Rise of the 'Fan-Sumer' Matter to Brands," web-strategist.com, November 6, 2007. Accessed at http://www.web-strategist.com/blog/2007/11/06/myspace-and-facebook-launch-new-advertising-products-why-hyper-targeting-social-ads-and-rise-of-the-fan-sumer%E2%80%9D-matter-to-brands/.
2. G. Malcolm Lewis, "Maps, Mapmaking, and Map Use by Native North Americans," chapter 4 of *The History of Cartography*, volume 2, book 3, *Cartography in the Traditional African, American, Arctic, Australian, and Pacific Societies*, ed. David Woodward and G. Malcolm Lewis (University of Chicago Press, 1998). Accessed at https://www.press.uchicago.edu/books/HOC/HOC_V2_B3/HOC_VOLUME2_Book3_chapter4.pdf.
3. Corinna Bremer and Scott Peterson, "China's Crazy Influencer Industry: A German Stands Out Amidst Clone Factories and Billion-dollar Revenues," OMR, September 24, 2018. Accessed at https://omr.com/en/china-influencer-marketing/.
4. Angela Doland, "China's Influencers Don't Just Push Brands—They Create Their Own," *AdAge*, February 7, 2018. Accessed at https://adage.com/article/digital/china-s-influencers-create-brands/312229.
5. Karen Freeman, Patrick Spencer, and Anna Bird, "Three Myths About What Customers Want," *Harvard Business Review*, May 23, 2012. Accessed at https://hbr.org/2012/05/three-myths-about-customer-eng.

Part One

1. Rochelle Bailis, "The State of Influencer Marketing: 10 Influencer Marketing Statistics to Inform Where You Invest," BigCommerce,

March 27, 2019. Accessed at https://www.bigcommerce.com/blog /influencer-marketing-statistics/#10-most-important-influencer -marketing-statistics-for-2019.

2. Erin Smith, "11x Higher ROI. Proven." TapInfluence, April 7, 2016. Accessed at https://www.tapinfluence.com/blog-11x-higher-roi-proven/.

3. 2019 Edelman Trust Barometer Special Report, "In Brands We Trust Accessed at https://www.edelman.com/sites/g/files/aatuss191/files /2019-07/2019_edelman_trust_barometer_special_report_in_brands _we_trust.pdf.

4. "How Big is Influencer Marketing in 2018?" Infographic. Infu-encerDB, November 21, 2018. Accessed at https://cdn2.hubspot.net /hubfs/4030790/MARKETING/Resources/Education/Infographic /InfluencerDB-State-of-the-Industry-2018.pdf.

Chapter 1

1. "How to Get a Celebrity Endorsement from the Queen of England," NPR, May 21, 2012. Accessed at https://www.npr.org/sections/money /2012/05/21/153199679/how-to-get-a-celebrity-endorsement-from -the-queen-of-england?t=1557830579947.

2. "The History of Staunton Chessmen," Staunton Chess Sets, 2012. Accessed at https://www.stauntonchesssets.com/staunton_history.html.

3. "Reading the Trade Cards," Museum of Health Care at Kingston. Accessed at http://www.museumofhealthcare.ca/explore/exhibits/trade -card/celeb3.html.

4. Annette Blaugrund, *Dispensing Beauty in New York and Beyond: The Triumphs and Tragedies of Harriet Hubbard Ayer* (Arcadia Publishing, 2011), p. 58.

5. Alejendro Benes, "Samuel Clemens and his Cigars," *Cigar Aficionado*, Winter 1995–96. Accessed at https://www.cigaraficionado.com/index .php/article/samuel-clemens-and-his-cigars-6042.

6. Rich Griset, "Where There's Smoke: Looking Back at a Time When Chesterfields Were King," *Chesterfield Observer*, June 1, 2016. Accessed at https://www.chesterfieldobserver.com/articles/where-theres -smoke-2/.

7. Jack Doyle, "Babe Ruth & Tobacco, 1920s–1940s," *The Pop History Dig*, September 25, 2010, updated June 23, 2016. Accessed at https://www.pophistorydig.com/topics/babe-ruth-tobacco-1920s -1940s/.

8. "History of Celebrity Endorsements in Advertising: From Doris Day to Liza Koshy to George Clooney," TagedStudio, January 24, 2019.

Accessed at https://tagedstudio.com/history-of-celebrity-endorsements-in-advertising-from-doris-day-to-liza-koshy-to-george-clooney/.

9. Alec Banks, "The Time Michael Jordan Was Forced to Wear Reebok," HighSnobiety, August 18, 2016. Accessed at https://www.highsnobiety.com/2016/08/18/michael-jordan-reebok/.

10. Jake Woolf, "Every Sneaker Kanye West Ever Designed, Ranked," *GQ*, June 8, 2017. Accessed at https://www.gq.com/gallery/kanye-west-sneakers-ranking.

11. Randall Beard, "Trust in Advertising—Paid, Owned and Earned," September 17, 2012, citing Nielsen Global Trust in Advertising Survey, Q3 2011. Accessed at https://www.nielsen.com/us/en/insights/article/2012/trust-in-advertising-paid-owned-and-earned/.

12. 2019 Edelman Trust Barometer Special Report, "In Brands We Trust?" Accessed at https://www.edelman.com/sites/g/files/aatuss191/files/2019-07/2019_edelman_trust_barometer_special_report_in_brands_we_trust.pdf.

13. Adam Fusfeld, Nike Golf Was Rewarded for Sticking with Tiger Woods," *Business Insider*, December 3, 2010. Accessed at https://www.businessinsider.com/tigers-nike-endorsement-proved-profitable-2010-12?IR=T.

14. Kelsie Rimmer, "The Stats Driving Influencer Marketing in 2019," Tribe, no date. Accessed at https://www.tribegroup.co/blog/the-stats-driving-influencer-marketing-in-2019?.

15. Marty Swant, "Twitter Says Users Now Trust Influencers Nearly as Much as Their Friends, *Adweek*, May 10, 2016. Accessed at https://www.adweek.com/digital/twitter-says-users-now-trust-influencers-nearly-much-their-friends-171367/.

16. Elizabeth Segran, "Female Shoppers No Longer Trust Ads or Celebrity Endorsements," Fast Company, September 28, 2015. Accessed at https://www.fastcompany.com/3051491/female-shoppers-no-longer-trust-ads-or-celebrity-endorsements.

17. Hayley Soen, "The Instagram Models and Influencers that Promoted the Fyre Festival Scam," The Tab, January 17, 2019. Accessed at https://thetab.com/uk/2019/01/17/fyre-festival-instagram-models-89928.

18. Celie O'Neil-Hart and Howard Blumenstein, "Why YouTube Stars Are More Influential Than Traditional Celebrities," Think with Google, July 2016. Accessed at https://www.thinkwithgoogle.com/consumer-insights/youtube-stars-influence/.

19. Tara Johnson, "11 Influencer Marketing Statistics That Will Impact Your Campaign in 2019," Tinuiti (formerly CPC Strategy), December

26, 2018. Accessed at https://www.cpcstrategy.com/blog/2018/12/influencer-marketing-statistics/.

20. Tereza Litsa, "Influencer Marketing 2019: Seven Key Stats You Need to Know," ClickZ, January 4, 2019. Accessed at https://www.clickz.com/influencer-marketing-2019-stats/223174/.

21. Audiense, *Influencer Marketing: Identify the Most Relevant Influencers for Your Audience.* ebook. Accessed at http://resources.audiense.com/ebooks/identify-the-most-relevant-influencers-for-your-audience.

22. Rachel Strugatz, "Digital Download: The Power of Influencer Referrals," WWD, September 19, 2017. Accessed at https://wwd.com/business-news/retail/influencers-chriselle-lim-man-repeller-leandra-medine-reward-style-drive-traffic-and-sales-10994073/.

23. Alissa Degreef, "Rakuten, 2019 Influencer Marketing Global Survey of Consumers," Rakuten Marketing blog, March 14, 2019. Accessed at https://blog.rakutenmarketing.com/insights/rakuten-marketing-2019-influencer-marketing-global-survey-report/.

24. Vikram Alexei Kansara, The Digital Iceberg," Business of Fashion, February 15, 2016. Accessed at https://www.businessoffashion.com/articles/fashion-tech/the-digital-iceberg-luxury-fashion-marketing.

Chapter 2

1. "Instagram Rich List 2019," HopperHQ, no date. Accessed at https://www.hopperhq.com/blog/instagram-rich-list/.

2. Peter Kafka and Rani Molla, "2017 Was the Year Digital Ad Spending Finally Beat TV, Vox, December 4, 2017. Accessed at https://www.vox.com/2017/12/4/16733460/2017-digital-ad-spend-advertising-beat-tv.

3. Kurt Wagner, "Digital Advertising in the US Is Finally Bigger Than Print and Television," Vox, Recode, February 20, 2019. Accessed at https://www.vox.com/2019/2/20/18232433/digital-advertising-facebook-google-growth-tv-print-emarketer-2019.

4. Dominick Sorrentino, "Email Marketing Generates the Highest ROI," Brafton, January 9, 2018. Accessed at https://www.brafton.com/news/content-marketing-news-2/digital-channel-profitable-33-marketers-arent-sure/.

5. Michael Gerard, "The Buyer's Journey Demystified by Forrester," Curata, 2014. Accessed at http://www.curata.com/blog/the-buyers-journey-demystified-by-forrester/.

6. Gerard, "The Buyer's Journey Demystified by Forrester."

7. "Top Sites in United States," Alexa.com, May 23, 2019. Accessed at https://www.alexa.com/topsites/countries/US.

8. Claudia Beaumont, "New York Plane Crash: Twitter Breaks the News, Again," *The Telegraph*, January 16, 2009. Accessed at https://www.telegraph.co.uk/technology/twitter/4269765/New-York-plane-crash-Twitter-breaks-the-news-again.html.

9. Katerina Eva Matsa and Elisa Shearer, "News Use Across Social Media Platforms, 2018," Pew Research Center, September 10, 2018. Accessed at http://www.journalism.org/2018/09/10/news-use-across-social-media-platforms-2018/.

10. Randall Beard, "Trust in Advertising—Paid, Owned, Earned," September 17, 2012, citing Nielsen Global Trust in Advertising Survey, Q3 2011. Accessed at https://www.nielsen.com/us/en/insights/article/2012/trust-in-advertising-paid-owned-and-earned/.

11. Mike Neumeier, "Branding by Trust: The Rise of the B2B Influencer," *Forbes*, October 2, 2017. Accessed at https://www.forbes.com/sites/forbescommunicationscouncil/2017/10/02/branding-by-trust-the-rise-of-the-b2b-influencer/#5315507651a6.

Chapter 3

1. Matt McGee, "EdgeRank Is Dead: Facebook's News Feed Algorithm Now Has Close To 100K Weight Factors," Marketing Land, August 16, 2013. Accessed at https://marketingland.com/edgerank-is-dead-facebooks-news-feed-algorithm-now-has-close-to-100k-weight-factors-55908.

Chapter 4

1. Salman Aslam, "Snapchat by the Numbers: Stats, Demographics & Fun Facts," Omnicore Agency, April 27, 2019. Accessed at https://www.omnicoreagency.com/snapchat-statistics/.

2. Danny Wong, "Facebook, Pinterest, Twitter, and YouTube Referrals Up 52%+ in Past Year," Shareaholic, October 15, 2013. Accessed at https://blog.shareaholic.com/social-media-traffic-trends-10-2013/.

3. Karla Gutierrez, "Studies Confirm the Power of Visuals in eLearning," Shift Disruptive eLearning, July 8, 2014. Accessed at https://www.shiftelearning.com/blog/bid/350326/studies-confirm-the-power-of-visuals-in-elearning.

4. "Maersk Line Wins Social Media Campaign of the Year Award," Safety4Sea, September 17, 2012. Accessed at https://safety4sea.com/maersk-line-wins-social-media-campaign-of-the-year-award/.

5. Rob Reed, "The Year of the Instagram Strategy," The Huffington Post, December 6, 2017. Accessed at https://www.huffingtonpost.com/max-gladwell/the-year-of-the-instagram_1_b_4171833.html.

6. "Sour Then Sweet Hijinks," Shorty Awards. Mondelez International, VaynerMedia. Accessed at http://shortyawards.com/7th/sour-then -sweet-hijinks.

7. Taylor Lorenz, "Instagram's Wannabe-Stars Are Driving Luxury Hotels Crazy," *The Atlantic*, June 13, 2018. Accessed at https://www .theatlantic.com/technology/archive/2018/06/instagram-influencers -are-driving-luxury-hotels-crazy/562679/.

Chapter 5

1. Randall Beard, "Trust in Advertising—Paid, Owned and Earned," September 17, 2012, citing Nielsen Global Trust in Advertising Survey, Q3 2011. Accessed at https://www.nielsen.com/us/en/insights /article /2012/trust-in-advertising-paid-owned-and-earned/.

Chapter 6

1. Alison Millington, "A Day in the Life of 26-Year-Old Kayla Itsines— The Most Influential Fitness Star on Earth—Who Has a 7-Million Strong Instagram Following," *Independent*, September 24, 2017. Accessed at https://www.independent.co.uk/life-style/life-kayla-itsines -most-influential-fitness-star-on-earth-million-instagram-following -blogger-a7964136.html.

2. Madeline Berg, "The Highest Paid YouTube Stars 2017: Gamer DanTDM Takes the Crown with $16.5 Million," *Forbes*, December 26, 2017. Accessed at https://www.forbes.com/sites/maddieberg/2017 /12/07/the-highest-paid-youtube-stars-2017-gamer-dantdm-takes -the-crown-with-16-5-million/.

3. Klear, "The State of Influencer Marketing 2019." Accessed at https:// klear.com/TheStateOfInfluencerMarketing2019.pdf.

4. Sabri Suby, "How HiSmile Grew from a Tiny $20k Investment to $40 Million eCommerce Powerhouse in 3 Years," King Kong. February 7, 2018. Accessed at https://kingkong.com.au/hismile-grew-tiny-20k -investment-40-million-ecommerce-powerhouse-3-years-detailed -case-study/.

5. "Instagram Marketing: Does Influencer Size Matter?" Markerly, April 11, 2016. Accessed at http://markerly.com/blog/instagram-marketing -does-influencer-size-matter/.

6. "Peers Have Influence Over Consumers, Celebrities Don't," Collective Bias, March 29, 2016. Accessed at https://www.collectivebias.com /post/blog-2016-03-non-celebrity-influencers-drive-store-purchases.

7. untitled case study video, IMAgency. Accessed at https://imagency .com/work/ah/.

8. Tanya Dua, "The LaCroix Guide to Tapping 'Micro-influencers,'" Digiday, May 18, 2016. Accessed at https://digiday.com/marketing /the-lacroix-guide-micro-influencers/.

9. Chris Anderson, "The Long Tail," *Wired*, October 1, 2004. Accessed at https://www.wired.com/2004/10/tail/.

Chapter 7

1. Nathan Egan, "Your Company Has Thousands of Websites, Not Just One. Social Business Optimization Will Help You Leverage Them All," PeopleLinx, January 17, 2013.

2. "2018 Edelman Trust Barometer," January 21, 2018. Accessed at https://www.edelman.com/trust-barometer.

3. James O'Gara, "Are You Underinvesting in the One Thing That Can Truly Drive Growth?" Itsonmessage.com, July 18, 2018. Accessed at https://www.itsonmessage.com/some-companies-win-others-lose/.

4. Aaron Smith and Monica Anderson, "Social Media Use in 2018," Pew Research Center, March 1, 2018. Accessed at https://www.pewinternet .org/2018/03/01/social-media-use-in-2018/.

5. Doug Kessler, "Employed Media: How Internal Advocates Can Share Your Content Marketing," Content Marketing Institute, March 24, 2014. Accessed at https://contentmarketinginstitute.com/2014/03 /employed-media-internal-share-content-marketing/.

6. Greg Shove, "Marketing That Money Can't Buy—Getting Employees to Tweet About Work," *Fast Company*, November 22, 2013. Accessed at https://www.fastcompany.com/3022068/marketing-that-money -cant-buy-getting-employees-to-tweet-about-work.

7. "Prudential Retirement Empowers Its Channel on LinkedIn," People Linx case study, 2013. Accessed at https://www.slideshare.net/BillConn l/people-linx-prudential-case-study.

8. Mindi Rosser, "5 Important Employee Advocacy Statistics," Smarp blog, March 9, 2017. Accessed at https://blog.smarp.com/5-important -employee-advocacy-statistics-to-remember.

9. Sarah Goodall, "My Favorite Employee Advocacy Statistics," Business 2 Community, March 30, 2015. Accessed at https://www.business2 community.com/social-selling/favorite-employee-advocacy-statistics -01193266.

10. Qubist blog, "How Iceland Foods Increased Brand Awareness and Growth Through Their Employee Advocates." September 20, 2017.

11. Dennis Owen, "What Does Managing Social Media In a Large Company Like Cathay Pacific Mean in Today's World?" Linkedin, August 29, 2015. Accessed at https://www.linkedin.com/pulse /what-does-managing-social-media-large-company-like-cathay -dennis-owen.

Chapter 8

1. Courtney Eckerle, "Inbound Marketing: How Influencers Grew Website Traffic 204% in Four Months for a Convenience Food Company," MarketingSherpa, July 20, 2017. Accessed at https:// www.marketingsherpa.com/article/case-study/influencers-grew -website-traffic.
2. David Griner, "Lord & Taylor Got 50 Instagrammers to Wear the Same Dress, Which Promptly Sold Out," *Adweek*, March 31, 2015. Accessed at https://www.adweek.com/brand-marketing/lord-taylor -got-50-instagrammers-wear-same-dress-which-promptly-sold-out -163791/.
3. "Lord & Taylor Settles FTC Charges It Deceived Consumers Through Paid Article in an Online Fashion Magazine and Paid Instagram Posts by 50 'Fashion Influencers,'" Federal Trade Commission press release, March 15, 2016. Accessed at https://www.ftc.gov/news-events/press -releases/2016/03/lord-taylor-settles-ftc-charges-it-deceived-consumers -through.
4. Imogen Watson, "Influencer Marketing Spend Grows 83%," The Drum, July 15, 2019. Accessed at https://www.thedrum.com/news /2019/07/15/influencer-marketing-spend-grows-83.
5. See my interview with Codrut Turcanu who specializes in the creation of roundup blog posts here: https://nealschaffer.com/influencer -marketing-roi-roundup-post/.
6. Tor Refsland, "How To Get 20,231 Views With One Epic Roundup Post (Step-By-Step)," Sumo, November 2, 2018. Accessed at https:// sumo.com/stories/epic-roundup-post.
7. Influencer Marketing by Shoutcart. Accessed at https://shoutcart.com/.
8. Onalytica case study. Accessed at https://performancein.live/static /img/downloads/onalytica-case-studies.pdf.
9. Saya Weissman, "GE and Instagram Want Aviation Fans to Take a Walk with Them," *Digiday*, September 4, 2013. Accessed at https:// digiday.com/marketing/ge-instagram-aviation/.
10. David Ciancio, "How to Host an Influencer Event at Your Restau- rant," Burger Conquest blog, January 8, 2018. Accessed at https://

burgerconquest.com/2018/01/08/how-to-host-an-influencer
-marketing-event-at-your-restaurant/.

11. Kristina Monllos, Why More Brands Are Adding Young Influencers
to Their Marketing and Creative Teams," *Adweek*, September 18,
2017. Accessed at https://www.adweek.com/brand-marketing
/why-more-brands-are-adding-young-influencers-to-their-marketing
-and-creative-teams/.

12. "Why Gary Vaynerchuk Is Putting His Name on a K-Swiss Sneaker,"
The Oracles, *Entrepreneur*, November 14, 2017. Accessed at https://
www.entrepreneur.com/article/304465.

13. Kaya Yurieff, "Amazon Wants Influencers to Help It Sell Clothes,"
CNN Business, June 5, 2019. Accessed at https://www.cnn.com
/2019/06/05/tech/amazon-influencers-shopping/.

Chapter 9

1. Neal Schaffer, *Maximize Your Social* (Hoboken, NJ: Wiley, 2013).

2. Relatable, "The 2019 State of Influencer Marketing Report." Accessed
at https://www.relatable.me/the-state-of-influencer-marketing-2019.

3. ACTIVATE, "2019 State of Influencer Marketing Study."

4. Arnaud Roy, "The State of Influencer Engagement in 2015," Launch
Metrics, June 18, 2015. Accessed at https://www.launchmetrics.com
/resources/blog/state-influencer-engagement.

5. Brendan Lowry, "Can't Afford a Kardashian, Use a Micro-Influencer,"
Curalate, August 19, 2016. Accessed at https://www.curalate.com
/blog/micro-influencer-brand-marketing/.

6. "Influencer Marketing Benchmark Report: 2019," Influencer Marketing Hub, May 28, 2019. Accessed at https://influencermarketinghub
.com/influencer-marketing-2019-benchmark-report/.

7. Influencer Marketing 2019 Industry Benchmarks," Mediakix, no date.
Accessed at https://mediakix.com/influencer-marketing-resources
/influencer-marketing-industry-statistics-survey-benchmarks/.

8. "The 2018 State of Influencer Marketing Study," Activate, 2018. Accessed at https://try.activate.social/2018-state-of-influencer-study/.

9. Alfred Lua, "How Much Does Social Media Influencer Marketing
Cost?" Buffer, April 4, 2018. Accessed at https://blog.bufferapp.com
/influencer-marketing-cost.

10. Instagram Influencer Sponsored Post Money Calculator, https://
influencermarketinghub.com/instagram-money-calculator/; Analyze
Any Instagram Account for Fake Followers and Engagements, https://
hypeauditor.com/.

11. "April 2017 Influencer Rate and Engagement Report," Influence.co blog, February 19, 2018. Accessed at http://blog.influence.co/instagram -influencer-rates/.

12. Cheryl Smithem, "Food and Beverage Content Marketing Case Stud-ies," The Balance Small Business, February 24, 2019. Accessed at https:// www.thebalancesmb.com/food-and-beverage-content-marketing-case -studies-1326358.

Chapter 10

1. J. Clement, "Distribution of Facebook Users in the United States as of January 2018, by Age Group and Gender," Statista, May 20, 2019. Accessed at https://www.statista.com/statistics/187041/us-user-age -distribution-on-facebook/.

2. "Age Distribution of Active Social Media Users Worldwide as of 3rd Quarter 2014, by Platform," Statista, November 17, 2014. Accessed at https://www.statista.com/statistics/274829/age-distribution-of -active-social-media-users-worldwide-by-platform/.

3. Nicholas Carlson, "The Real History of Twitter," *Business Insider*, April 13, 2011. Accessed at https://www.businessinsider.com/how -twitter-was-founded-2011-4.

4. Claudia Beaumont, "New York Plane Crash: Twitter Breaks the News, Again," The Telegraph, January 16, 2009. Accessed at https://www .telegraph.co.uk/technology/twitter/4269765/New-York-plane-crash -Twitter-breaks-the-news-again.html.

5. Samantha Murphy, "Twitter Breaks News of Whitney Houston Death 27 Minutes Before Press," Mashable, February 12, 2012. Accessed at https://mashable.com/2012/02/12/whitney-houston-twitter/.

6. David Shepardson, "Facebook's Zuckerberg to Testify Before Con-gress: Source," Reuters. March 27, 2018. Accessed at https://www .reuters.com/article/us-facebook-cambridgeanalytica-britain/facebooks -zuckerberg-will-not-appear-before-uk-parliament-committee -media-idUSKBN1H3121; "Facebook CEO Zuckerberg Called to Testify Before UK-Canadian Committee," Associated Press, October 31, 2018. Accessed at https://www.bnnbloomberg.ca/u-k-canadian -grand-committee-seeks-to-question-zuckerberg-1.1160983.

7. Case study provided in interview with agency.

8. Kristen Matthews Twitter page, https://twitter.com/KristenWords/.

9. "Deming the Man," The W. Edwards Deming Institute. Accessed at https://deming.org/deming/deming-the-man.

10. "The State of Influencer Marketing 2019: Benchmark Report," Influ-encer Marketing Hub.

11. "Tiny Armies Game Influencer Case Study," Game Influencer. Accessed at https://gameinfluencer.com/wp-content/uploads/2017/12/Tiny-Armies-GameInfluencer-Case-Study.pdf.
12. Case Studies page. Accessed at https://www.relatable.me/case-studies.
13. "Case Study: 2017 @SalvationArmyUS #FightForGoodTour," Fight for Good Tour, Team Strub blog, February 14, 2018. Accessed at http://www.teamstrub.com/single-post/2018/02/14/Case-Study-2017-SalvationArmyUS-FightForGoodTour.

Chapter 11

1. "CLIF Kid Case Study," CLEVER. Accessed at https://www.realclever.com/case-study/clif-kid/.
2. Amy Watson, "Average Number of *The Big Bang Theory* Viewers in the United States as of May 2019, by Season (In Millions)," Statista, June 6, 2019. Accessed at https://www.statista.com/statistics/607266/big-bang-theory-viewers-season/.
3. Brendan Lowry, "Can't Afford a Kardashian, Use a Micro-Influencer," Curalate, August 19, 2016. Accessed at https://www.curalate.com/blog/micro-influencer-brand-marketing/.
4. "Bumble Bee Seafoods: Blogger Outreach," Fandom Marketing. Accessed at https://fandommarketing.com/knowledge-center/finding-perfect-influencer-for-your-brand/.
5. Andrea Johnson, "Inbound Marketing: How Influencer Marketing Attracted 100,000 Website Clicks to Luxury Mattress Site," Marketing Sherpa, March 31, 2016. Accessed at https://www.marketingsherpa.com/article/case-study/how-influencer-marketing-attracted-website-clicks.
6. Arthur Hilhorst, "Two Methods to Find the Perfect Influencers," Onalytica, July 30, 2014. Accessed at www.onalytica.com/blog/posts/influencer-identification-two-methods-to-find-the-perfect-influencers/.
7. "See How Hawaii's Tourism Campaign Wins Big on Instagram," Mediakix, May 12, 2016. Accessed at https://mediakix.com/blog/instagram-marketing-case-study-hawaii-tourism-campaign/.

Chapter 12

1. Edgar Alvarez, "Influencer Luka Sabbat Sued for Not Shilling Snapchat Spectacles on Instagram," *Entrepreneur*, November 1, 2018. Accessed at https://www.entrepreneur.com/article/322672.
2. Adam Sutton, "Social Media Marketing: GNC's Strategy for Courting Online Influencers and Adding 383,000 Facebook Fans," Marketing

Sherpa, February 9, 2012. Accessed at https://www.marketingsherpa
.com/article/case-study/gncs-strategy-courting-online-influencers.

3. "What Makes Influencers Want to Work with Brands?" Carusele,
November 4, 2015. Accessed at https://blog.carusele.com/makes
-influencers-work-with-brands.

4. Keegan Shoutz, "TapInfluence Unveils No. 1 Thing Motivating Social
Influencers When Working with Brands, and It's Not Money," *Business Wire*, November 10, 2016. Accessed at https://www.businesswire
.com/news/home/20161110005789/en/TapInfluence-Unveils-No
.-1-Motivating-Social-Influencers.

5. "Altimeter and TapInfluence Release the Influencer Marketing Manifesto; Studies of Both Marketers and Influencers Uncovers How to
Succeed in the New Social Capital Paradigm," Venturebeat, July 26,
2016. Accessed at https://venturebeat.com/2016/07/26/altimeter
-and-tapinfluence-release-the-influencer-marketing-manifesto-study
-of-both-marketers-and-influencers-uncovers-how-to-succeed
-in-the-new-social-capital-paradigm/.

6. Dionsios Favata, "How Micro-Influencers Are Upending the Traditional Advertising Model," *Forbes*, June 8, 2017. Accessed at https://
www.forbes.com/sites/forbesnonprofitcouncil/2017/06/08
/how-micro-influencers-are-upending-the-traditional-advertising
-model/#7197543a39aa.

7. FTC website, September 2017. Accessed at https://www.ftc.gov/policy
/international/ftc-international-monthly/september-2017.

8. "A HASHOFF State of the Union Report," Hashoff, April 2017.

9. "Altimeter and TapInfluence Release the Influencer Marketing Manifesto."

10. "What Makes Influencers Want to Work with Brands?"

11. Johnny Lieu, "NBA Draft No. 1 Pick Markelle Fultz Could Use
Some Work on His Paid Instagram Post Game," Mashable, June 23,
2017. Accessed at https://mashable.com/2017/06/23/markelle-fultz
-instagram-post/.

12. Alysha Tsuji, "Deandre Ayton Latest to Make Comical Error of Forgetting to Edit a Sponsored Post," *USA Today*, June 20, 2018. Accessed at https://ftw.usatoday.com/2018/06/deandre-ayton-nba-draft
-sponsored-tweet-mistake-social-media-post-funny-oops.

Chapter 13

1. Jimmy Doheny, "How JClub Drove $16K in Sales and Achieved
550% ROI with Micro-Influencers on Dealspotr," Dealspotr blog.

Accessed at https://dealspotr.com/article/jclub-micro-influencer -marketing-case-study.

2. "The Forrester New Wave: Influencer Marketing Solutions, Q4 2018," Forrester, December 11, 2018. Accessed at: https://www.forrester .com/webinar/The+Forrester+New+Wave+Influencer+Marketing+ Solutions+Q4+2018/-/E-WEB26807.

Chapter 14

1. Jacques Bughin, "A New Way to Measure Word-of-Mouth Marketing," *McKinsey Quarterly*, April 2010.
2. "2014 Influencer Marketing Benchmarks Report," Burst Media, March 2015. Accessed at http://intelligence.communicatieonline.nl /sites/default/files/80fa_burstmedia_2014_influencer_marketing _benchmarks_report.pdf.
3. Patrick Coffee, "Study: Influencer Marketing Pays $6.50 for Every Dollar Spent," *Adweek*. March 26, 2015. Accessed at https://www .adweek.com/digital/study-influencer-marketing-pays-6-50-for -every-dollar-spent/.

Chapter 15

1. Mathew Ingram, "Here's Why Trust in Media Is at an All-time Low," *Fortune,* September 15, 2016. Accessed at https://fortune.com/2016 /09/15/trust-in-media/.
2. Suzanne Kapner, "Inside the Decline of Sears, the Amazon of the 20th Century," *The Wall Street Journal*, October 31, 2017. Accessed at https://www.wsj.com/articles/inside-the-decline-of-sears-the-amazon -of-the-20th-century-1509472095.
3. Robinson Meyer, "Mark Zuckerberg Says He's Not Resigning," *The Atlantic*, April 9, 2018. Accessed at https://www.theatlantic.com /technology/archive/2018/04/mark-zuckerberg-atlantic-exclusive /557489/.
4. Jakob Nielsen, "The 90-9-1 Rule for Participation Inequality in Social Media and Online Communities," Nielsen Norman Group. October 9, 2006. Accessed at https://www.nngroup.com/articles/participation -inequality/; Charles Arthur, "What Is the 1% Rule?" *The Guardian*, July 19, 2006. Accessed at https://www.theguardian.com/technology /2006/jul/20/guardianweeklytechnologysection2.
5. Jacques Bughin, "Getting a Sharper Picture of Social Media's Influ- ence," McKinsey, July, 2015. Accessed at https://www.mckinsey.com

/business-functions/marketing-and-sales/our-insights/getting-a-sharper
-picture-of-social-medias-influence.

6. Richard Fry, "Millennials Are the Largest Generation in the U.S. Labor Force," FactTank, Pew Research Center, April 11, 2018. Accessed at http://www.pewresearch.org/fact-tank/2018/04/11/millennials-largest-generation-us-labor-force/.

7. "What Is the Social Proof Theory?" The Psychology Notes HQ, August 31, 2015. Accessed at https://www.psychologynoteshq.com/social-proof/.

Chapter 16

1. Mike Neumeier, "Branding by Trust: The Rise of the B2B Influencer," Forbes, October 2, 2017. Accessed at https://www.forbes.com/sites/forbescommunicationscouncil/2017/10/02/branding-by-trust-the-rise-of-the-b2b-influencer/#5315507651a6.

2. Cory Wainwright, "Why Blog? The Benefits of Blogging for Business and Marketing," HubSpot, September 30, 2015. Accessed at https://blog.hubspot.com/marketing/the-benefits-of-business-blogging-ht.

3. Nicholas Confessore and Gabriel J. X. Dance, "Battling Fake Accounts, Twitter to Slash Millions of Followers," The New York Times, July 11, 2018. Accessed at https://www.nytimes.com/2018/07/11/technology/twitter-fake-followers.html.

4. Christopher Wilson, "Trump Mad Over Losing Twitter Followers, White House Confirms," Yahoo News, April 24, 2019. Accessed at https://www.aol.com/article/news/2019/04/24/trump-mad-over-losing-twitter-followers-white-house-confirms/23716640/.

5. Kevin Roose, "Don't Scoff at Influencers. They're Taking Over the World," The New York Times, July 16, 2019. Accessed at https://www.nytimes.com/2019/07/16/technology/vidcon-social-media-influencers.html.

Chapter 17

1. David Cohen, "Facebook Officially Launches Lookalike Audiences," Adweek, March 19, 2013. Updated article accessed at https://www.adweek.com/digital/lookalike-audiences/.

2. Meghan Graham, "Fake Followers in Influence Marketing Will Cost Brands $1.3 Billion This Year, Report Says," CNBC, July 24, 2019. Accessed at https://www.cnbc.com/2019/07/24/fake-followers-in-influencer-marketing-will-cost-1point3-billion-in-2019.html.

INDEX

ABOUT THE AUTHOR

NEAL SCHAFFER is an international authority on helping businesses through their digital transformation of sales and marketing through consulting, training, and helping enterprises large and small develop and execute on social media marketing strategy, influencer marketing, and social selling initiatives. Founder of the marketing consultancy PDCA Social, Neal also teaches marketing to executives at Rutgers Business School and the Irish Management Institute. Fluent in Japanese and Mandarin Chinese, Neal is a popular global keynote speaker and has been invited to speak on four continents in more than a dozen countries, including conferences such as CES, CEBIT, MarketingProfs B2B Forum, Content Marketing Conference, and Social Media Marketing World. He is also the author of three other books on social media, including *Maximize Your Social*. With an engaged online audience of nearly half a million people, Neal is a sought-after thought leader to brands and celebrities worldwide.